The Dominant Firm
A Study of Market Power

Research in
Business Economics and
Public Policy, No. 5

Fred Bateman, Series Editor

Chairman and Professor
Business Economics & Public Policy
Indiana University

Other Titles in This Series

The Dominant Firm
A Study of Market Power

by
Alice Patricia White

UMI RESEARCH PRESS
Ann Arbor, Michigan

Produced and distributed by
UMI Research Press
an imprint of
University Microfilms International
Ann Arbor, Michigan 48106

Library of Congress Cataloging in Publication Data

White, Alice Patricia.
The dominant firm.

(Research in business economics and public policy ;
no. 5)
Revision of thesis—Yale University, 1980.
Bibliography: p.
Includes index.
1. Industrial concentration—United States. I. Title.
II. Series.

HD2785.W45 1983   338.8'2'0973   83-5001
ISBN 0-8357-1444-6

Contents

List of Tables

List of Figures

List of Figures

1

Introduction

The "dominant firm" as a theoretical concept dates from 1930.[1] In the half century which has elapsed it has been discussed by succeeding generations of economists and has eventually made its way into industrial organization textbooks.[2] Although originally a theory about price leadership, it has developed along a number of lines, and a variety of behaviors are now associated with dominant firms. They include pricing at a level which deters all entry and varying price, and hence market share, as part of a long-run profit maximization strategy.[3] Not all of the hypothesized behavioral patterns are compatible. Some research provides examples of actual firm behavior which coincides with predicted behavior, but by and large the dominant firm is a theoretical construct.[4] The goal of this research is to empirically evaluate the dominant firm market structure.

Two broad themes will characterize this investigation. First, what are the sources of dominance? We shall seek to discover pre-conditions for the development of the dominant firm market structure. Our concern is with the growth of the structure rather than just its behavior once it is in existence. We view dominance as a condition requiring constant regeneration. As such, we shall investigate the persistence of a dominant firm structure in some industries and not in others. Second, given that dominant firm structures exist, are similar patterns of conduct observed across the various dominant firm industries, and is this the behavior theory predicts? If there is a dominant firm market structure rather than individual dominant firms, we expect to observe parallels in the conduct of the various firms. Dominant firm structures may arise from diverse sources and yet behave similarly. Alternatively, each source of dominance may be associated with unique behavioral patterns. Certain conduct may also tend to perpetuate the dominant firm structure through feedbacks from behavior to structure which enable the firm to control to some extent the evolution of the market structure.

These issues will be explored in the following chapters by means of statistical and case studies of a sample of firms. The discussion will be organized in the following manner. The remainder of this chapter will contain a discussion of the concept of dominance and a review of the economic and legal literature to suggest possible sources of dominance and behavioral patterns. In chapter 2 some of these behavioral patterns will be examined in the context of statistical comparisons of dominant and non-dominant firms. The method of analysis in chapters 3-6 will be a comparative case study of a sample of firms. Chapter 3 will contain an analysis of their sources of dominance, and chapters 4 and 5 will be concerned with price and non-price behavior, respectively. The direct and indirect effects of behavior on structure will be examined in chapter 6. The final chapter will contain a summary and conclusions.

Definition of Dominance

The first step in a study of the dominant firm market structure is to develop a definition of "dominance." One method is to choose some numerical index of market share. For example, Oliver Williamson has suggested that a firm with a market share of sixty percent or more is dominant.[5] Others have set their sights lower—fifty percent[6] or, in the case of Stigler, forty percent, unless the second largest firm is also "big."[7] Stigler added the caveat to his definition to avoid duopoly situations, but he did not specify how much "larger" the dominant firm's share need be.

Use of a numerical index to identify a dominant firm market structure has the advantage of precision and avoids the criticism that choices are ad hoc. However, the precision of choices based upon market share is dependent upon the precision with which such shares are measured. Firm specific market share data are difficult to obtain, but aside from that, there are problems related to the quality of such measures. Actual firms participate in many markets; in some they may be dominant while in others they may not. Ideally, we would like share information for each product a firm makes, but such data are not generally available. Alternatively, firms are assigned to broad product categories. Their shares are then determined on the basis of their proportion of employees or sales. This method of determining market share necessarily obscures dominance of individual products. The quality of the data now depends upon the relevance of the assignment of the product category.

Because of the difficulty of getting data which is firm specific and because of problems with the quality of that data, an alternative means of identifying "dominance" will be developed. The term "dominance" implies a difference in the position or influence of individuals within an association. One method of identifying a dominant firm structure is to focus on the nature of this disparity of influence. In *Webster's New Collegiate Dictionary* one definition of a "dominant" organism is

> ...any of one or more kinds of organism (as a species) in an ecological association that exerts a controlling influence on the environment and thereby largely determines what other kinds of organisms share in the association.[8]

Webster's New Collegiate Dictionary, (Springfield, MA: G. & C. Merriam, Co. ca. 1975), p. 339.

The market is the association in which firms operate; the degree of competition may be interpreted as the environment. A dominant firm structure is thus one in which a firm is able to control to a degree the competitive environment in which all other firms operate. This firm's actions will shape the market outcome without the consent of others. This test of dominance may be distilled into two questions. First, does the firm have some means of controlling the competitive environment? Traditional theory would ask if the firm has the power to determine price or output. An affirmative answer does not imply the firm has complete control; it does imply the firm is partially free of oligopolistic restraints. Second, can the firm's policies determine the nature of the market association itself? The type of product the dominant firm produces may determine what constitutes the market. The firm may direct technical progress or set product quality standards that affect the ability of others to compete with new products.

The first condition is sufficient for "dominance" in the traditional sense of the term; the second condition implies a broader approach. It is a view of dominance over time and as it evolves. It suggests that in the long-run the market power of firms is reflected in their ability to affect the product as much, if not more so, than their power over price.

This method of defining dominance is not completely outside the tradition of economic literature. F. Zeuthen, in *Problems of Monopoly and Economic Warfare,* wrote the following of "partial monopoly," another term for a dominant firm structure:

> A partial monopoly exists when one enterprise has so much power in the market that it is to its interest to charge a price which exceeds costs, even if sales are reduced thereby, whilst at the same time there are other enterprises which at each price have certain different sales irrespective of the policy of other firms, the monopoly included. This is often the case where by the side of one very large enterprise there are many smaller ones, which for a long time will be unable to extend their production, and perhaps will not be allowed to do so by the larger concern.[9]

Similarly, F. Machlup wrote:

> A firm may be called dominant—in connection with price policy—when it is...so large compared with all other firms in the industry that it is not seriously affected by the actions of the small ones and allows them to do as they please.[10]

Tradition is broken by focusing on variables, other than price, that a firm can control. Likewise, the approach we are suggesting is broader than the one implicit in price leadership and limit pricing models, yet it includes these situations. Price leaders are not subject to strategic oligopolistic behavior. Although they do not have complete freedom, constraint in the form of the fringe supply is predictable. Their pricing policy determines the market outcome. Limit pricing models can be interpreted as a description of the response of a dominant firm facing expansion by the fringe. In this instance as well, the dominant firm is able to choose a combination of price and number of competitors and hence is able to determine its competitive environment.

Aside from the problems of measuring market share, our approach is more suited to handling dynamic notions of dominance, that is, how the market power of the firm changes over time. If entry is either open or partially blocked, a firm's future market share is dependent upon current price levels. The dominant firm may vary market share over time in order to maximize the discounted value of its profits.[11] This type of analysis assumes that price policies are the major way in which a dominant firm alters the competitive environment of other firms, but a dominant firm may function also by changing the product itself. For example, it may determine the direction of product development through its research policies. Our approach is also better suited to handle the multiproduct dominant firm. If a dominant firm makes two complementary products, A and B, and there is a fringe of firms making B, the dominant firm is able to alter the competitive environment in the market for B whenever it changes characteristics of A that affect their joint use. Thus, the share of the dominant firm in market B alone would not accurately reflect its ability to shape the market outcome.

Sources of Dominance

An objective of this research is to provide insights into the development of the dominant firm structure. A review of the economic literature below will suggest sources of market power and hence dominance. In addition to the economic literature, some of the ideas will be drawn from legal cases involving dominant firms. Although courts frequently focus upon abusive conduct, some decisions have dealt with the legality of market power per se. Theories relating to the origins of dominance are embodied in the tests for monopolization framed in these decisions. An extensive review of the legal treatment of dominant firms will be deferred until later in this chapter. Consider first the sources of dominance.

Economies of Scale

The dominant firm may be the first firm which was able to realize economies of scale. The existence of a fringe of smaller firms in the long-run may imply several things. The residual demand curve may be such that entry is still possible at a small scale and lower price. The fringe firms may not make the same product as the dominant firm; they may produce specialized items or serve special markets. Finally, antitrust laws may constrain the dominant firm from driving out the fringe firms.

Superior Skill, Business Acumen

> A single producer may be the survivor out of a group of active competitors, merely by virtue of his superior skill, foresight and industry...[12]

One way to interpret this is to apply a "great person" argument to economic events. That is, there are unique individuals with exceptional talents who appear erratically and influence the growth of a firm. George Eastman of Eastman Kodak or Thomas Watson of International Business Machines might be such individuals. Without the influence of these leaders a different market structure might have developed.

Predation or Exclusionary Tactics

A dominant firm might establish its position through tactics that drive competitors out of the market. The classic example is pricing below marginal cost. Alternatively, it may employ tactics that are not predatory but, nevertheless, hamper the ability of other firms to compete. Such tactics are labeled exclusionary. In another section of the *U.S. vs. Alcoa* decision Learned Hand wrote:

> ...we can think of no more effective exclusion than progressively to embrace each new opportunity as it opened, and to face every newcomer with new capacity already geared into a great organization...[13]

Natural Advantages

Unique location is an example of one type of natural advantage. This argument is analogous to the one for superior skill except that it is applied to physical inputs rather than managerial talents. Control of a vital input may be considered a natural advantage, or it may be considered a predatory device. American Metal Climax is an example of a firm which may be said to have a natural advantage. It is this country's leading producer of molybdenum.[14] Approximately ninety percent of its output comes from one mine near Climax, Colorado.

Mergers

Now carefully screened, mergers are less important in the creation of dominance than they once were. They may, however, be important as an original source of dominance now being maintained by other means. A merger that has been successfully upheld in court can be interpreted as a legally protected source of dominance. In *United States vs. United Shoe Machinery*

(1954), Judge Wyzanski held that one of the sources of United's power was the original constitution of the company, a merger of several shoe machinery manufacturers.[15] This merger had been upheld by the Supreme Court in an action that constituted a legal license according to Wyzanski.[16]

Patents

Patents also may be considered legally protected dominance, but their protection is of limited duration. One effect of patents is to give the firms holding them different and possibly lower cost technologies. Like mergers, they may function as an initial source of dominance that is maintained by other methods. Patents are one indicator, albeit imperfect, of the extent to which dominant firms are innovators. Their importance as a source of dominance will provide some evidence concerning the significance of dominant firms as innovators or quick imitators.

Historic Accident

Learned Hand also suggested dominance may be a result of an accident or the ineptitude of rivals.[17] A formal description of dominance due to "accident" in economic theory is the stochastic view of firm growth. Scherer has demonstrated that concentration is generated even by starting with equal size firms and letting the firms' growth rates in each period be a random draw uncorrelated with past growth rates.[18] Hand suggested that sudden changes in tastes or costs that drive all but one firm from the market fall into this category.[19] He had in mind exogenous cost and taste changes outside the control of any firm.

Product Loyalty

Loyalty may be generated by actual or perceived product differences. Actual differences include product standardization or quality control and the type of service facilities offered. Perceived differences are related to "image," perhaps created through advertising. Regardless of the cause of loyalty, it can be an important source of market power and hence dominance.

Efficiency

Efficiency is included as a source of dominance to cover cost differences not attributable to economies of scale, superior skill, natural advantages, or patents. Some firms may have lower costs as a result of learning effects or better motivation of their labor force.

An aim of our research is to evaluate the importance of the above-mentioned sources of dominance in the experience of actual firms, but we are also interested in the persistence of dominance in some industries and not in others. Dominance may arise from one source and be maintained by another. We hypothesize that the original source of a firm's dominance affects its persistence. For example, dominance due to patents will not be as durable as dominance achieved through superior skill or efficiency. In chapters 2-6 we shall examine this hypothesis in the framework of a comparative case study of dominant firms. Some of the older firms in the sample achieved their position by merger. Our hypothesis implies that dominance achieved by such means will not be as durable as that achieved within the boundary of the firm. In addition, since mergers are now circumscribed, dominance is more likely to depend upon internal factors and may be longer lived.

The sources and persistence of dominance may also be a function of the type of good produced. The products of this sample of dominant firms fall roughly into two groups: branded consumer goods whose purchase represents a small portion of a single consumer's budget and technologically complex goods, both producer and consumer. The markets for technologically complex goods are more subject to change and flux than the markets of differentiated consumer goods. In situations of flux, dominance may be easy to establish due to patents or to being the first firm to achieve economies of scale or simply to lower costs. Alternatively, this business climate may attract leaders of unusual ability. However, the situations of change that give rise to dominance may also increase the difficulty of maintaining it. For producers of consumer goods, product loyalty may be of more importance as a source of dominance. Loyalty is not easy to create, but once in existence it has a long lifespan. Thus, we hypothesize that dominance will be easier to establish in technologically complex goods but easier to maintain in consumer goods. One mitigating factor is the ability of dominant firms to control the direction of change within their industries. In such a case, change might facilitate maintenance of dominance.

Behavioral Patterns of Dominant Firms

Given that a firm is dominant, several common patterns of behavior are likely to be observed. The existence of these patterns will be explored in the statistical analysis of chapter 2 and in the case studies.

Price Setter

The earliest discussions of dominant firms are found in the context of price leadership models. They predict that the dominant firm subtracts the fringe supply from the industry demand curve to derive its own demand curve and maximizes profit by setting price where marginal revenue equals marginal cost. The fringe firms "follow" this price; they face rising marginal costs so they cannot expand, but their demand is completely elastic at the price set by the dominant firm.

Entry Deterring Behavior

Limit pricing models traditionally have been used to describe the behavior of a group of colluding oligopolists facing entry, but they may also be used to describe the response of a dominant firm facing expansion by the fringe. The predicted behavior of the dominant firm is also price setting, but price setting at a level that does not allow the fringe to earn supra-normal profit. The level of price will be a function of costs of the fringe after expansion, estimates of demand made by the fringe, and estimates of the share of the market captured after expansion.[20] It is generally assumed that the lowest attainable cost of the fringe firms is greater than that of the dominant firm.

Excess capacity may be another device for deterring entry or expansion. In a passage cited above, Learned Hand accused Alcoa of always facing newcomers with new capacity.[21] Michael Spence has developed a model in which capacity rather than price is used as the device to constrain the fringe. Excess capacity is held in a pre-entry period and then output is expanded and price reduced whenever entry or expansion is threatened. The behavior predicted in this model as opposed to a limit pricing model would be

> ... the presence of capacity above cost minimizing levels, given output ... [and] in a dynamic context, capacity running well ahead of demand ... [22]

This analysis as well as that of limit pricing models and price setting models assumes that the product is homogeneous. Spence has extended his analysis to any investment which reduces the prospects of the entrant. In an industry with differentiated products, this may be advertising or marketing activities.

Investment Policies and Their Financing

Schumpeter hypothesized that monopolies may "prove to be the easiest and most effective way of collecting the means by which to finance additional investment."[23] Dominant firms, if their market power does lead to higher profit, could be expected to have more internal funds to use for investment. The simple availability of funds is not the entire issue, however. The firms' actual investment policies may be another behavioral characteristic that distinguishes them. Building ahead of demand was discussed earlier. The ability to determine the direction of innovation was alluded to in the discussion of the sources of dominance. Certainly the type of investment that a firm makes, particularly the amount devoted to research and development or advertising, is an important issue.

Diversification

Diversification into other industries is one way to achieve stability of earnings. We hypothesize that dominant firms will have policy instruments available to achieve stability without resorting to diversification. The impetus to diversify may also be a function of the dynamics of the industry. If dominant firm industries have a greater potential for growth this may also condition the urge to diversify.

If diversification occurs we hypothesize that it will be largely product extension. This will allow marketing knowledge and technical expertise to be used and product loyalty to be transferred.

A Review of Legal Decisions Involving Dominant Firms

Many dominant firms have been cited for anti-trust violations, particularly under Section 2 of the Sherman Act. In grappling with the legality of dominant firms' market power, courts have considered the sources of that power and the reasons for its persistence. A review of previous legal decisions will augment the earlier discussion of the sources of dominance and provide a background for policy recommendations regarding anti-trust treatment of dominant firms.

Dominant firms are, by definition, possessors of a degree of market power, however, Section 2 of the Sherman Act focuses on "monopolizing" conduct rather than the mere fact of holding market power:

> Every person who shall monopolize or attempt to monopolize or combine or conspire with any other person or persons to monopolize any part of the trade or commerce among the several States, or with foreign nations, shall be deemed guilty of a misdemeanor.[24]

The use of the active verb "monopolize" rather than a condemnation of market power itself has resulted in a tension in the law concerning the treatment of dominant firms. The hesitation to condemn monopoly power outright indicates the framers of the law felt some market power may be inevitable. The origin of market power will thus be an important consideration in anti-trust cases involving dominant firms.

The passage cited above was not originally part of Senator Sherman's bill but was added by the Judiciary Committee. At the time, the lawmakers were concerned primarily with combinations or trusts. The generality of the provision which became Section 2 was debated since the members of the Judiciary Committee felt there might be such a thing as innocent monopolists who had not achieved their power by means of restraints of trade.

Mr. Kenna...[Section 2] if plain English means anything...provides a penalty for...any citizen...who happens by his skill and energy to command an innocent and legitimate monopoly of a business...

Mr. Hoar...I think all the other members of the committee agreed...that "monopoly" is a technical term known to the common law...which has a clear and legal signification, and it is this: It is the sole engrossing to a man's self by means which prevent other men from engaging in fair competition with him...I suppose, therefore...that a man who merely by superior skill and intelligence...got the whole business because nobody could do it as well as he could was not a monopolist, but that it involved something like the use of means which made it impossible for others to engage in fair competition, like the engrossing, the buying up of all other persons engaged in the same business. [25]

The framers of the Sherman Act thus saw two sources of market power. One was the combination or trust which involved "...the buying up of all other persons engaged in the same business." At the same time they recognized that there might be an "innocent" monopolist. That is, market power might be the result of superior skill and intelligence.

The divergent views concerning the sources of market power did not stop with Judiciary Committee debates about the Sherman Act. The draftsmen were in a sense conferring upon the federal courts a jurisdiction to apply a common law regarding monopolization. This branch of common law, like all others, is in a continual process of change. As the law developed we observe other implicit theories about the sources of market power. The following discussion will be a roughly chronological review of legal decisions. It is not intended as an exhaustive review of Section 2 cases but rather an indication of the evolution of what constitutes "monopolization." In the course of the review we hope to discover the legal view of the origins of market power.

The lawmakers who fashioned the Sherman Act were obviously most concerned about combinations that resulted in trade restraints, and this colored the earliest interpretations of the law. Market power flowed from restraints of trade, and the protection of the right of the individual to contract was sufficient to prevent monopoly power from evolving. Mr. Chief Justice White, writing in one of the early landmark cases *Standard Oil Co. vs. United States,* explained the purposes of the second section:

...consideration of the text of the second section serves to establish that it was intended to supplement the first and to make sure that by no possible guise could the public policy embodied in the first section be frustrated or evaded...In other words, having by the first section forbidden all means of monopolizing trade that is, unduly restraining it by means of contract, combination, etc., the second section seeks, if possible, to make the prohibitions of the act all the more complete and perfect by embracing all attempts to reach the end prohibited by the first section, that is, restraints of trade... [26]

This opinion implies there are only two sources of dominance—combination or merger and restraints of trade or predation. As White wrote, "...the freedom of the individual right to contract when not unduly or improperly exercised was the most efficient means for the prevention of monopoly." [27]

However, the court had not yet begun to grapple with the notion of monopoly power created by an individual firm without the use of predatory devices. Harking back to the problem raised by Mr. Kenna in the debate over Section 2, Chief Justice White noted

> ... that nowhere at common law can there be found a prohibition against the creation of monopoly by an individual ... After all, this is but an instinctive recognition of the truisms that the course of trade could not be made free by obstructing it and that the individual's right to trade could not be protected by destroying such right.[28]

Market power held by an individual and not the result of trade restraints was thus not a concern of anti-trust enforcers. Given the premise that protection of the right to contract was the most efficient means of preventing monopoly, this was a consistent idea. Market power gained by the individual through exercising the right to contract could not itself be attacked without destroying the right to contract. This foreshadows a later decision in which Learned Hand noted that "The successful competitor, having been urged to compete, must not be turned upon when he wins."[29]

The focus on the right to contract is continued in *United States vs. American Tobacco Co.* American Tobacco's market power was ascribed to other methods than the " ... exertion of the ordinary right to contract and to trade."[30] In particular, these involved trade wars, " ... the gradual absorption of control over all the elements essential to the successful manufacture of tobacco products ... ," and the extraction of promises not to compete on the part of manufacturers who were purchased.[31] The *American Tobacco* case broke new ground in one respect; the idea was introduced that what are otherwise lawful practices may be unlawful if undertaken by a firm with monopoly power.[32] This is the beginning of a tradition in which certain actions in conjunction with market power are viewed differently from those actions alone. Given the notion that monopoly power may be created by the individual legally, it implies higher standards of conduct if the persistence of market power is to be judged legal.

Following these decisions were a series of cases in which the issue of the legality of size itself was considered. In *United States vs. United States Steel Corporation* the majority concluded that size alone was not an offense. Day, writing for the minority, agreed that

> ... the act offers no objection to the mere size of a corporation, nor to the continued exertion of its lawful power, when that size and power have been obtained by lawful means and developed by natural growth, although its resources, capital and strength may give to such corporation a dominating place in the business and industry with which it is concerned.[33]

Once more we encounter the theme of legal market power if it is not acquired by unlawful exclusionary methods. Exactly what constitutes "natural growth" was left undefined.

The legality of size was reiterated in *United States vs. International Harvester Co. et al.*[34] This case is interesting because the nature of the firm's distribution system was an issue. As part of the relief, International Harvester was limited to one sales agent in any town even though it produced two competing lines, McCormick and Deering. It was constrained in a way which its other competitors were not. The *International Harvester* decision introduced selling conditions as opposed to simply the production of goods as an issue in market power consideration. The form of the relief also reiterated the idea begun in *American Tobacco* that otherwise lawful actions of a firm in conjunction with market power may be illegal.

The *United States vs. Aluminum Co. of America* case was a departure from this tradition that emphasized combinations, trade restraints, and exclusionary behavior. In his decision, Learned Hand suggested that a firm which has an overwhelming share of the market monopolizes whenever it does business even if there is no showing of exclusionary behavior. He softened his stand somewhat by suggesting the origin of monopoly may be crucial in determining its legality.

> Nevertheless, it is unquestionably true that from the very outset the courts have at least kept in reserve the possibility that the origin of a monopoly may be critical in determining its legality... This notion has usually been expressed by saying that size does not determine guilt; that there must be some "exclusion" of competitors; that the growth must be something else than "natural" or "normal;" that there must be a "wrongful intent" or some other specific intent; or that some "unduly" coercive means must be used.[35]

His ensuing discussion of the origins of market power as a legal defense provide us with several additional theories concerning the sources of dominance. For example, a firm may be the unwitting recipient of market power without having tried to put an end to competition. Such would be the case if economies of scale were so large relative to the market that one plant could meet all demand. Alternatively, Judge Hand suggested that changes in taste or cost may drive all but one firm from the market. Hand also reviewed the suggestion that a single survivor may owe his or her position to "...superior skill, foresight and industry..."[36]

Although acknowledging that the origin of market power may be important in determining legality, Hand went on to base his decision on the dynamic competitiveness of the market. Alcoa, according to Hand, had every instrument necessary for market dominance and had the will to take advantage of new opportunities. It anticipated competition and forestalled it. It stimulated demand but not without "...making sure it could supply what it had evoked."[37] Alcoa doubled and redoubled its capacity.

> ...we can think of no more effective exclusion than progressively to embrace each new opportunity as it opened and to face every newcomer with capacity already geared into a great organization, having the advantage of experience, trade connections and the elite of personnel.[38]

Hand was thus addressing the issue of the dynamic sources of market power, that is, how dominance is renewed and persists over time. He interpreted Alcoa's actions as dynamically exclusionary. In a situation similar to that found in *American Tobacco* and *International Harvester,* a lawful action by a firm without market power may be construed as being exclusionary when taken by a firm with market power.

In *United States vs. United Shoe Machinery Corp.* the court attempted to deal further with "exclusionary" actions as a source of market power.[39] District Judge Wyzanski, writing in that case, recognized that he was now facing a situation that the legislators who wrote the Sherman Act had not faced, that is,

> ...the intermediate case where the causes of an enterprise's success were neither common law restraints of trade, nor the skill with which the business was conducted, but rather some practice which without being predatory, abusive or coercive was in economic effect exclusionary.[40]

In writing this, he thus made explicit the court's view that market power may result from sources other than trade restraints or superior skill. He elaborated on Judge Hand's review of the sources of market power and suggested that to escape liability, the defendant

> ...must bear the burden of proving that its share of the market was attributable to its ability, natural advantages, legal license, or perhaps to others' lack of interest in entering the market.[41]

Ability was construed to include superior skill or products and economic or technological efficiency. Natural advantages included accessibility to raw materials or markets. Legal licenses were those conferred by and used within the limits of the law. They included patents or franchises granted by a public authority.

In United's case in particular, Wyzanski ruled that its sources of power included the original constitution of the company and the superiority of its products and services. The former was judged above reproach since the original constitution of the company was found lawful by the Supreme Court.[42] United's activities that were in "economic effect exclusionary" included the leasing system, a practice which had been traditional in the shoe machinery industry since the Civil War, its acquisition of patents, and its activities in selling shoe factory supplies. Judge Wyzanski attributed United's power to "... the magnetic ties inherent in its system of leasing, and not selling, its more important machines... While the law allows many enterprises to use such practices, the Sherman Act is now construed by superior courts to forbid the continuance of effective market control based in part upon such practices."[43] Once again, we observe a concern with distribution practices when a firm has a degree of market power. Judge Wyzanski felt that in one sense the leases were "natural and normal," however, "not the inevitable consequences of ability, natural forces, or law."[44]

Throughout the history of the Sherman Act courts have examined the origin of market power in determining its legality. The earliest cases involved combinations and restraints of trade. These sources of market power were ruled illegal. Monopoly power established through individual effort, however, was not. Size itself was not an offense as long as it was obtained through natural growth.

As the common law surrounding the Sherman Act developed, the courts began to broaden their view and to consider the legality of certain firm actions given that the firm had market power but had obtained it legally. In the *Alcoa, United Shoe,* and *International Harvester* cases, otherwise lawful business practices were construed as being exclusionary in the presence of market power. This aspect of the law is still in a state of flux.

Conclusion

The prevailing legal position on dominant firms at this time is to consider first, whether the origins of their market power are "legal" and second, whether discretionary firm behavior serves to perpetuate that power. Both of these issues will be examined in the remaining chapters. The experiences of a sample of firms will provide insights into the relative importance of various factors in the development of market power and thus the accuracy of the concepts of market power on which legal decisions are based. An examination of firm conduct will further suggest what behavior, if any, serves to protect the position of the firms and whether anti-trust activity should be directed more toward this behavior.

2

Statistical Investigation

The dominant firm has been identified as one whose actions will shape the market outcome without the consent of others, but how is this dominance reflected in various observable firm characteristics? What, if anything, is peculiar about them? Dominant firms by virtue of their size are unique within their industries, but are there any characteristics that distinguish them from large firms in general? The discussion in chapter 1 indicated possible structural and behavioral differences between non-dominant and dominant firms. We shall examine samples of dominant and non-dominant firms and test whether various measures of their behavior and balance sheets differ.[1] This type of analysis cannot reveal the original sources of a firm's dominance, nevertheless, because we view dominance as a condition constantly being recreated, it may provide insights into its maintenance. Finally, characteristics not common to large firms in general will illuminate those behavioral patterns of dominant firms to be examined later.

Following a discussion of the sources of data, a series of statistical tests will be conducted. They are of two types. First, we examine the equality of several variables for samples of dominant and non-dominant firms during the years 1958 to 1977. The tests were conducted separately for every year in the sample. Unless indicated otherwise, all tests were two-sided. An ordinary t-test for the equality of mean levels of two variables assumes that these variables have equal variances. If this hypothesis was rejected, the subsequent test of means was conducted assuming inequality of variances. It is only an approximate t-test. The reported levels of significance reflect the joint significance of the sequential tests. This is followed by some standard profitability-concentration studies which take explicit account of dominance and estimate its effect upon firm profitability independent of that of concentration.

Sample Selection and Description of Data

Lists of dominant firms are available from two sources: Wilcox and Shepherd's *Public Policies Toward Business*[2] and an article by Leonard Weiss, "The

Concentration-Profits Relationship and Antitrust."[3] The firms mentioned in these two sources are given in table 1. A third source has been used to supplement this list. In "The Elements of Market Structure," William Shepherd developed firm specific market share measures for a number of large firms.[4] Using his data, we selected a list of firms according to a variant of the Stiglerian definition of dominance. Firms were included if they had a market share of at least forty percent or twice the size of the next largest firm, whichever was greater. The latter condition was added to avoid duopoly situations.[5] Neither Wilcox and Shepherd nor Weiss provide explicit criteria for their choice of firms. Wilcox and Shepherd do offer market share estimates, and their choices meet the criterion of market share greater than or equal to forty-five percent. The firms included in our sample are also indicated in table 1. Only five firms occur on all lists.

We excluded firms for a number of reasons. General Electric, Coca-Cola, Kellogg, the *New York Times,* and Time Inc. were omitted because we felt their market structures were more accurately characterized as duopoly or oligopoly. Knight Newspapers and Rayonier have subsequently been involved in mergers. American Photocopy's market situation has changed greatly; as early as 1968, Shepherd estimated its market share had declined to 20 percent. A case can be made for the dominance of the remaining firms.[6] Caterpillar, Ethyl, Timkin, Joy Manufacturing, and United Aircraft have been excluded because their competitive situation is in sufficient flux to render their dominance at least questionable.

Comparing our sample with the one generated from Shepherd's data and Stigler's definition, it is evident that an explicit market share definition is a rough approximation of the one we are advocating. We included two firms (Xerox, Procter and Gamble) which did not meet the market share criteria,[7] and one (Boeing) for which Shepherd made no estimate. We excluded four firms (Time, Coca-Cola, Rayonier, American Photocopy) which strict market share criteria suggested.

Firm financial reports are the original source of the information used in the following statistical tests. They are available on the COMPUSTAT industrial file produced by Standard and Poor. This data tape contains information on a large number of companies traded on the New York and American Stock Exchanges. The control sample of large non-dominant firms was randomly drawn from manufacturing companies listed on the COMPUSTAT primary industrial file which specifically includes all companies in the S&P 400. We limited our attention to the primary industrial file in order to have similar size distributions of firms within both samples. Both the dominant firm sample and the control sample have the same mean level of sales and assets, although the dominant firms have a higher variance of both variables. Because all of the dominant firms were engaged in manufacturing, the control sample has been similarly limited. Sample statistics are given in an appendix.

Table 1. Lists of Dominant Firms

Dominant Firm	Wilcox & Shepherd (1973)*	Weiss (1960-1970)*	Shepherd (1961)*	Sample
General Motors (autos, locomotives, buses)	x		x	x
IBM (computers, typewriters)	x	x	x	x
Western Electric (telecommunication equipment)	x	x		
General Electric (heavy electrical equipment)	x			
Eastman Kodak (photographic supplies)	x	x	x	x
Xerox (copying equipment)	x	x		x
Procter & Gamble (detergents)	x			x
United Aircraft (aircraft engines)	x			
Coca-Cola (flavoring syrups)	x		x	
Campbell Soup (canned soup)	x	x	x	x
Polaroid (instant cameras)	x		x	x
Gillette (razors)	x	x	x	x
Kellogg (dry cereals)	x			
Times Mirror (newspaper)	x	x	x	x
New York Times (newspaper)	x			
Various drug firms (drugs)	x			
Caterpillar Tractor (tractors, heavy equipment)		x		
Boeing (commercial aircraft)		x		x
Ethyl (anti-knock compounds)		x		
Timkin (roller bearings)		x		
Joy Manufacturing (coal mining equipment)		x		
Knight Newspapers (newspaper)		x		
William Wrigley, Jr. (chewing gum)		x	x	x
CPC International (corn refining products)			x	x
Time Inc. (magazines)			x	
Avon Products (cosmetics)			x	x
Hershey (chocolate, cocoa products)			x	x
Rayonier (dissolving pulps)			x	
Pitney Bowes (postage meters, mailing equipment)			x	x
American Photocopy (photocopying equipment)			x	

* Years covered in the study.

A Comparison of Dominant and Non-Dominant Firms

Both price leadership models and limit pricing models predict more than competitive profits. Leonard Weiss in "The Concentration-Profits Relationship and Antitrust" examined after tax profit as a percentage of equity as a suggestive test of the dominant firm hypothesis.[8] He found that average profit rates, 1960-70, for the dominant firms in his sample exceeded that of the average for all manufacturing. This difference was significant at the 5% level. Our results also indicate higher rates of return for dominant firms. The mean level of after tax rate of return on assets was higher for dominant firms in every year, 1958-77, as reported in table 2.[9] The level of significance was 5% or less, that is, in some years the difference was significant even at a 1% or .5% level. Nineteen seventy-four was the one exception. The after tax rate of return on equity produced similar results except that in three years the mean levels did not differ significantly.[10]

Investors in dominant firms appear to earn significantly higher rates of return, but they do not appear to pay for this in terms of higher variability of profit. In a test of the variance of after tax rates of return on assets reported in table 3, dominants do not differ significantly from non-dominants. Examining the rate of return on equity in a one-sided test, the variance of non-dominants is significantly greater than that of dominants at a 10% level.

The higher profits of dominant firms are a potential source of internal funds for further investments. Schumpeter recognized their possible importance in the oft-cited passage that monopolies may "prove to be the easiest and most effective way of collecting the means by which to finance additional investment."[11] Leverage indicates the mix of internal and external funds a firm has chosen to finance its investment projects. We examined the value of equity/assets for dominant and non-dominant firms. This variable is the inverse of leverage in the traditional sense; higher values of equity/assets imply lower leverage and vice versa. Prior to 1969, dominant and non-dominant firms did not differ significantly in their degree of leverage. However, between 1969 and 1977, dominant firms were significantly less leveraged. We thus find support for the Schumpeterian hypothesis in the capitalization policies of dominant firms. The movement in the leverage ratio of dominants vis-à-vis non-dominants may be interpreted in two ways. It is unlikely that there has been an increase in the overall risk of dominant firms leading to lower optimal levels of leverage. More likely profit expectations in the earlier period motivated debt financed expansion, and the economic climate of the seventies led to the cessation of these activities and more conservative policies.

We reported earlier that dominant firms have a lower variance of rate of return on equity. This result is probably attributable to the lower leverage of dominant firms since the variance of rate of return on assets was not significantly different, either.

Table 2.　Comparison of Dominant Firms and a Sample of Large Non-Dominant Firms*

Variable	Results
After tax rate of return on assets	The value of dominants exceeded that for non-dominants in every year. The difference was significant in 14 years at the 1% level, in 5 years (60-62, 67, 69) at the 10% level, and in one year (74) was not significant.
After tax rate of return on equity	The value for dominants exceeded that for non-dominants in every year. The difference was significant in 11 years at the 1% level, in 5 years (60, 65, 72, 73, 75) at the 5% level, in one year (66) at the 10% level, and in three years (69, 74, 76) was not significant.
Leverage measured as equity/assets	The value for dominants exceeded that for non-dominants in the years 1963-77. The difference was significant at the 10% level or less 1969-77. From 1958-1962 the value for non-dominants exceeded that for dominants but the difference was not significant.
R&D expenses as a proportion of sales. Data available 1970-77	The value for dominants exceeded that for non-dominants in every year. The difference was significant 1974-76 at the 10% level or less.
Advertising expenses as a proportion of sales. Data available 1971-77	The value for dominants exceeded that for non-dominants in every year. The difference was significant in 1972, 1973, 1975-77 at the 10% level or less.
Capital expenditures as a proportion of assets	The value for dominants exceeded that for non-dominants in every year. The difference was significant in the years 1962, 1963, 1966, and 1969-71 at the 10% level or less.

*　Equality of mean levels of the following variables was tested for each year 1958-77. All tests were two-sided.

Another issue concerning the investment policies of dominant firms is the type of investment they make. For this reason both research and development expenses and advertising expenses were examined. In the case of R&D expenses, data were available for the years 1970-1977. R&D expenses as a proportion of sales were higher for dominant than for non-dominant firms; the difference was significant for the years 1974-1976 at the 10% level or less. Many firms may consider R&D expenses discretionary and, therefore, cut them first

Table 3.   Variances for Dominant and Large Non-Dominant Firms
Comparison*

Variable	Results
After tax rate of return on assets	The values were not significantly different.
After tax rate of return on equity	The variance for dominant firms was significantly less than that of non-dominants in a one-sided test at the 10% level.
R&D expenses as a proportion of sales	The values were not significantly different.
Advertising expenses as a proportion of sales	The values were not significantly different.
Capital expenditures as a proportion of assets	The values were not significantly different.

*   For each firm the variances of the following variables were computed. Their mean levels were tested for equality across the samples of dominant and non-dominant firms. All tests were two-sided unless indicated otherwise.

in any austerity moves. We tested the variability of R&D expenses for dominant and non-dominant firms but could not reject the hypothesis of equality.

Advertising is a method of investing in product loyalty, one possible source of dominance. Dominant firms revealed higher proportions of advertising expenses to sales in all years for which data were available, and the difference was significant in every year but 1971 and 1974.

The ratio of capital expenditures to assets was examined to provide a rough test of Spence's hypothesis that firms use capacity as a limiting device. In six of the twenty years dominant firms exhibited significantly higher levels of investment per unit of assets. This is a rough indication that firms with market power do invest more in capacity, but the same result could have been generated if dominant firms have lumpy technologies which require investments in big chunks of capital while non-dominant firms can spread their expenditures more evenly. If dominant firms do have lumpier technologies we would expect it also to be reflected in a higher within firm variation of capital expenditures/assets. Consequently, we tested the equality of variances of (capital expenditures/assets) for dominant and non-dominant firms and could not reject the null hypothesis of equality. This strengthens the evidence for the former interpretation that dominant firms invest in capacity at higher rates than non-dominants.

A final hypothesis that we can examine here concerns the degree of diversification of dominant firms relative to non-dominants. We hypothesized that dominants would have fewer acquisitions. Betty Bock accumulated data on acquisitions by the 200 largest industrial firms between 1955 and 1968.[12] She presents data on the number of acquisitions totaling more than $10 million in reported assets. Eleven dominant firms from our sample were also included in her sample. In a one-sided test that the mean number of acquisitions of dominant firms is less than that of non-dominants, dominant firms were observed to have significantly fewer acquisitions at the 10% level.

A Comparison of Dominant Firms Based Upon Product Type

We noted in chapter 1 that, in this sample, dominant firms' products are of two types: differentiated, small-purchase consumer items and technologically complex goods—both producer and consumer. To examine the effect of product type on the behavior of dominant firms, the sample was divided into these two groups; table 4 indicates the way in which firms were classified. An analysis similar to that mentioned for dominant versus non-dominant firms was carried out for the two types of dominant firms. The results are presented in table 5.

Rate of return on assets differs significantly only in 1975, however, in every year producers of branded goods had higher mean profit rates than producers of technologically complex goods. The results for rate of return on equity are comparable. For rate of return on assets the within firm variance was not statistically different across product type, but for rate of return on equity, producers of branded goods had a significantly lower variance in a one-sided test at the 10 percent level.

We had no a priori hypotheses concerning leverage for a comparison between types of dominant firms. The tests indicate no significant difference.

Research and development expenses and advertising expenses displayed the pattern we would expect. Technologically oriented firms had significantly higher levels of R&D expenditures. Although the firms producing branded goods displayed higher levels of advertising, the difference was significant in no year. If advertising is the main tool for the creation of product loyalty, both types of dominant firms seem to be doing equal amounts.

In six years the technological firms had significantly higher levels of capital expenditures per unit of assets. They may be using capacity as an entry deterring device more frequently than the consumer type firms, or they may have technologies which require lumpier investment decisions. A test across product types of equality of the within firm variance of (capital expenditures/assets) indicates that technologically-oriented firms do have significantly higher variances; this evidence supports the lumpier investment theory.

In addition to examining the variance of capital expenditures, we examined the variance of advertising expenses and the variance of R&D expenses. The results are reported in table 6. The within firm variance of R&D

Table 4. Classification of the Sample by Product Type

Branded Consumer Goods	Technologically Complex Goods
Procter & Gamble	IBM
Campbell Soup	Xerox
Gillette	General Motors
Times Mirror	Kodak
William Wrigley, Jr.	Polaroid
CPC International	Boeing
Avon Products	Pitney Bowes
Hershey	

Table 5. Comparison of Dominant Firms Based Upon Product Type*

Variable	Results
After tax rate of return on assets	The value for DCON exceeded that for DHITEC in every year. The difference was significant in 1975 at the 10% level.
After tax rate of return on equity	The value for DCON exceeded that for DHITEC in all years but 1964-66. The difference was significant in 1975 at the 10% level.
Leverage measured as (equity/assets)	The value for DCON exceeded that for DHITEC in the years 1958-67, 1969-71, and 1977. In no year was this difference significant.
R&D expenses as a proportion of sales. Data available 1970-77	The value for DHITEC exceeded that for DCON in every year. The difference was significant at the 5% level in 1973-77 and at 10% in 1970 and 1972. In 1971 it was not significant.
Advertising expenses as a proportion of sales. Data available 1971-77	The value for DCON exceeded that for DHITEC in every year. The difference was not significant in any year.
Capital expenditures as a proportion of assets	The value for DHITEC exceeded that for DCON in every year. The difference was significant at the 10% level or less in 1958-60, 1965-66 and 1968.

* Equality of mean level of the following variables was tested for each year 1958-77. "DCON" denotes dominant firms producing branded items for consumers. "DHITEC" denotes dominant firms producing high technology items, either producer or consumer.

expenses per unit of sales did not differ significantly by product type; however, the variance of advertising expenses per unit of sales did. Producers of branded products had substantially higher variances than technology-based firms. This implies a pattern of advertising "blitzes" which may be associated with the introduction of new goods or a response to competitors' actions.

Table 6. Variances for Product Type Dominant Firm Comparison*

Variable	Results
After tax rate of return on assets	The values were not significantly different.
After tax rate of return on equity	The variance for DCON was significantly less than that for DHITEC in a one-sided test at the 10% level.
R&D expenditures as a proportion of sales	The values were not significantly different.
Advertising expenditures as a proportion of sales	The variance for DHITEC was significantly less than that for DCON in a one-sided test at the 1% level.
Capital expenditures as a proportion of assets	The variance for DHITEC was significantly higher than that for DCON in a one-sided test at the 5% level.

* For each firm the variances of the following variables were computed. Their mean levels were tested for equality across the division of the sample of dominant firms based upon product type. "DCON" denotes dominant firms producing branded items for consumers. "DHITEC" denotes dominant firms producing high technology items, either producer or consumer.

A Comparison of Dominant and Non-Dominant Firms Based Upon Product Type

In order to increase our understanding of the product-type split of dominant firms, we have also compared dominant firms producing branded products with large non-dominant firms of that type and similarly for technological dominant firms. The results are given in tables 7 and 8. Both groups of dominants continued to have higher profit rates on assets than the non-dominants, but the results for the branded product firms were much stronger. For them the difference was significant in sixteen years, while for the technological firms it was significant in only seven years. Results for the rate of return on equity are similar.

In the seventies, both types of dominant firms continued to be less leveraged. The technological dominant firms do significantly more R&D than similarly oriented non-dominants, but they do not do significantly more advertising. Interestingly, the branded products dominant firms do not do significantly more advertising than the non-dominants. If their dominance is a result of product loyalty, it does not require high levels of advertising to

Table 7.   Comparison of Dominant Firms Producing Branded Items for
Consumers and Non-Dominant Firms Producing Products of a Similar
Type*

Variable	Results
After tax rate of return on assets	The value for dominants exceeded that for non-dominants in every year. The difference was significant in 10 years at the 1% level; 2 years (68, 76) at the 5% level; and 4 years (61, 62, 67, 77) at the 10% level. It was not significant in 1965, 1969, 1970, and 1974.
After tax rate of return on equity	The value for dominants exceeded that for non-dominants in every year but 1976. The difference was significant in 12 years at the 5% level or less, and in 3 year (69, 74, 77) at the 10% level. It was not significant in 1959-60, 1967, 1972, or 1976.
Leverage measured as equity/assets	The value for dominants exceeded that for non-dominants in every year. It was significant in 1966 and 1973 at the 10% level.
R&D expenses as a proportion of sales. Data available 1970-77	The value for dominants exceeded that for non-dominants in every year. The difference was not significant in any year.
Advertising expenses as a proportion of sales. Data available 1971-77	The value for dominants exceeded that for non-dominants in every year. The difference was not significant in any year.
Capital expenditures as a proportion of assets	The value for dominants exceeded that for non-dominants in 15 years. It was significantly higher in 1971 at the 5% level.

*   Equality of mean levels of the following variables was tested for each year 1958-77. All tests were two-sided.

maintain. Within the technological product class, dominant firms have higher ratios of capital expenditures to assets, the difference being significant in eight of twenty years. For the other class of firms, this was true in only one year.

Dominance and the Concentration-Profits Relationship

One of the conclusions of the preceding research is that the type of concentration in a market may matter in terms of its effect on profitability. Previous studies of the concentration-profits relationship have generally

Table 8.   Comparison of Dominant Firms Producing High Technology
Products and Non-Dominant Firms Producing Products of a Similar
Type*

Variable	Results
After tax rate of return on assets	The value for dominants exceeded that for non-dominants in every year. The difference was significant 1962-68 at the 10% level or less.
After tax rate of return on equity	The value for dominants exceeded that for non-dominants in every year. The difference was significant 1961-68 at the 5% level and in 1958 at the 10% level.
Leverage measured as equity/assets	The value for dominants exceeded that for non-dominants 1967-77. The difference was significant 1973-77 at the 10% level or less.
R&D expenses as a proportion of sales. Data available 1970-77	The value for dominants exceeded that for non-dominants in every year. The difference was significant 1974-77 at the 1% level or less.
Advertising expenses as a proportion of sales. Data available 1971-77	The value for dominants exceeded that for non-dominants 1972-77. The difference was never significant.
Capital expenditures as a proportion of assets	The value for dominants exceeded that for non-dominants in every year. The difference was significant in 1959, 1962-63, 1965-67, 1969 and 1977 at the 10% level or less.

*   Equality of mean levels of the following variables was tested for each year 1958-77. All tests were two-sided.

disregarded this fact.[13] One exception is an article by Bradley Gale, "Market Share and Rate of Return" which considers the interactions between share and concentration.[14] Share is, however, a rough proxy for dominance. We will consider the effect "type" of concentration has when it is introduced as a dominance variable in concentration-profit studies.

With one exception the data used in this analysis were taken from the COMPUSTAT tapes. Concentration ratios were drawn from Shepherd's study "The Elements of Market Structure." Shepherd's data are for 1961 and are available for a smaller number of firms than are the COMPUSTAT data. In addition, a number of Shepherd's firms no longer exist as separate entities, and some are simply not located on the COMPUSTAT tapes. The sample which resulted from merging these two data sources was biased towards pharmaceutical, oil, and steel companies. For the ensuing analysis a sample was used which reflects the 1961 distribution of industries within the top 500 firms in terms of sales. Within industry groups the selection of firms was random.

Consider a simple model which relates the rate of return on equity to concentration and controls for size, leverage, and the possibility of non-linearities in the concentration variable. Size is measured by the natural log of assets, leverage by the ratio of equity to assets. Concentration is entered as a squared term. The results are shown in table 9. The f test indicates the simultaneous significance of all coefficients, but the estimate of the standard error of the regression is so large that it is impossible to separate the individual effects of the variables. Concentration is just barely insignificant—it would have been significant at the 11 percent level. Only the coefficient of log of assets is significant, and it is significantly negative. This is not surprising since our sample is drawn entirely from the top five hundred firms in terms of sales. The introduction of a dummy variable for dominance decreases the unexplained variation enough to allow the effects of the individual variables to be determined. Now concentration and dominance are observed to have significant, positive effects on profitability at the 10 percent level. Size remains significantly negative.

These results may at first appear to be a puzzle. If dominance is highly correlated with concentration, the act of explicitly introducing it would, if anything, be expected to decrease concentration's level of significance. But dominance is not merely a proxy for concentration. The correlation coefficient between concentration and dominance in this sample is only 0.4. The form which market power takes has an important effect on profitability. Measures such as the four-firm concentration index or even the Herfindal index cannot discriminate between market power in the form of an oligopoly or a dominant firm. This may explain the failure on the part of some researchers to find a significant relationship between concentration and profits. Leonard Weiss's review of concentration-profit studies reveals a number of such occasions. They include studies by Stigler,[15] Singer,[16] Brozen,[17] and Ornstein.[18] In the first three, no other control variables were introduced. In the last, no variable similar to type of concentration was introduced.

The act of explicitly introducing dominance modestly altered some of the coefficient estimates. The coefficient of concentration increased 11.9% and that of size decreased 10.6%. The effect of leverage increased 12.2%.

We have also argued that dominance may be "packaged" in different ways. Dominance may be found in branded products and rooted in consumers' loyalty. It also may be the result of innovation and hence located in products subject to a high degree of technical change. To test this hypothesis we have entered separate dummy variables for each type of dominance. The results are given in table 9; both variables are significant. A test of equality of the coefficients of the two types of dominance reveals that the effect of branded consumer goods dominance on profit is significantly greater than that of technologically-oriented dominance at the 10% level.

Table 9.   Dominance and Concentration-Profitability Studies

Dependent Variable	After tax rate of return on equity		
Independent Variables	Coefficient estimates (standard error)		
Intercept	.01448 (.06784)	.01441 (.06461)	.01396 (.06406)
Four-Firm Concentration Ratio	.00319 (.00198)	.00357* (.00189)	.00352* (.00188)
Log (assets)	-.00753* (.00432)	-.00833** (.00412)	-.00782** (.00410)
Leverage	-.00615 (.03835)	-.00540 (.03653)	-.00695 (.03623)
Concentration Squared	-.00001 (.00002)	-.00002 (.00001)	-.00002 (.00001)
Dominance		.05282*** (.01459)	
Branded Goods Dummy			.07456*** (.01915)
Technological Goods Dummy			.03276* (.01854)
F Ratio	6.821 (4,118)	8.639 (5,117)	7.822 (6,116)
R^2	.1878	.2696	.2880

* Significant at 10% level.
** Significant at 5% level.
*** Significant at 1% level.

If the model containing the dominance dummy variable is evaluated with D = 0 and other variables are set equal to their mean levels for the non-dominant sample, a profit level of .103 is predicted. This same model, evaluated with D = 1 and the other variables set equal to their mean levels for the sample of dominant firms, predicts profitability of .170. A ten percent increase in the mean level of concentration, taking into account the negative effect of the concentration squared term only leads to an increase in profit of .011. Actual rates of return on equity for another sample of firms in 1961 were .100 for non-dominant firms and .184 for dominants. The model does not quite capture the total increase in profits associated with dominance.

Conclusion

The preceding analysis has provided a preliminary sketch of the dominant firm market structure. We have identified a group of dominant firms and demonstrated that they have higher profit rates than non-dominants. We hypothesized that innovation or product loyalty were possible sources of dominance, and the dominant firms exhibited significantly higher levels of this type of "investment" through higher levels of R&D and advertising expenditures. Over part of the time period we studied, dominant firms were significantly less leveraged than non-dominants—support for the Schumpeterian hypothesis. We also found suggestive evidence to support the Spence hypothesis. Our theories related to diversification were substantiated.

Type of dominance also seems to matter. Branded product dominant firms have higher profits than similarly situated non-dominants or technological dominants. This type of dominance contributed significantly more to profit in our concentration-profit studies. The results of examining advertising expenses were ambivalent. Although dominant firms had higher levels of advertising than non-dominants, dominant firms producing branded products did not have significantly higher levels than technology based dominant firms, nor did they do significantly more advertising than similar non-dominants. The technologically oriented dominant firms, on the other hand, exhibited significantly more research and development expenditures than other dominants and technology oriented non-dominants. Both types of dominant firms had significantly higher levels of capital expenditures per unit of assets than the same type of non-dominants.

Our analysis also included an examination of dominance in the context of concentration-profitability studies. Dominance did not prove to be merely a proxy for concentration. The form in which concentration manifests itself has a significant effect on profitability. Explicitly introducing a dominance variable improved the explanatory power of the regression as did distinguishing the "type" of dominance.

The format of this analysis left several hypotheses to be investigated. In particular, we have evidence concerning only the maintenance of dominance and behavioral patterns rather than the original sources of dominance. They will be examined in the context of case studies of groups of dominant firms in the following chapters.

3

The Acquisition of Dominance

Two objectives of this research are to examine the basis of dominant firms' market power and the reasons for the persistence of that power in some firms but not others. These questions will be examined in the context of a comparative case study of a sample of dominant firms. In this chapter we shall consider the original acquisition of dominance, and in the following chapters we shall examine the behavioral patterns of dominant firms.

The creation of one market structure rather than another is not handled well in economic theory. Discussion centers around "market failures" that prevent competition from arising, carrying within it a presumption that a competitive market structure would occur naturally if not for these failures. Because of the crudeness of theory we shall limit our investigation to an examination of factors or combinations of factors which facilitate the acquisition of dominance. No attempt will be made to speculate upon the structure that would have evolved in their absence. We shall, however, be interested in determining the relative importance of "active" and "passive" sources of dominance. Passive sources of dominance are those which are technologically or legally grounded, such as economies of scale or patents. Economies of scale, in particular, imply that the market structure may be the result of a "state of nature." Active sources of dominance are the result of some strategic move on the part of the firm; they include invention, mergers, or the creation of product loyalty. The relative importance of active and passive factors in the creation of market power is of considerable interest from a policy standpoint. Active dominance may be prevented by injunction, while efforts to prevent dominance that is passive may simply be an attempt to alter the laws of nature.

The discussion will be organized in the following manner. First, the choice of firms and the sources of data will be reviewed. Second, several possible sources of dominance will be examined and the importance of each in the experiences of the firms will be evaluated. Third, we shall summarize the sources of dominance and examine whether these factors have changed over time. In addition, the sample will be divided on the basis of product type, and we shall investigate whether the factors creating dominance vary in a systematic way and whether dominance is easier to establish in one group as opposed to another.

The usual approach in economic research is to consider "the product" as that item which is the output of the manufacturing operations of a firm. Although one of our concerns in this chapter is the technological aspects of production, our conception of the product is not so limited. Consumers are not interested simply in a machine, the computer, but rather the services which flow from that device. Similarly, they are interested in pictures rather than photographic film per se. Aspects of a product, such as how it is marketed and the availability of replacement parts and service, define the product in the eyes of the consumer as much if not more so than the technical aspects of its production. When we examine possible sources of dominance we shall, for example, look at distribution and post-sale service as well as production. The origins of dominance may lie as often in the marketing skills and distribution facilities of firms as in the technology of production.

Selection of Firms

The sample includes firms that have recently acquired a dominant position, firms that were dominant in the early twentieth century and have since declined, and firms that were able to maintain their dominance from that time until the present. This choice of firms will provide insights into whether the sources of dominance have changed over time and whether some sources of market power are more durable than others. The sample has also been chosen so as to provide a mixture of firms producing high technology items and branded consumer items. Table 10 lists the firms in the sample according to "age" of dominance. The newly dominant firms are Boeing, IBM, and Procter & Gamble. In each case these firms held substantial market power in related products before their acquisition of dominance. Although the products themselves were related, there was a radical shift in the technology of production in each case. We have thus distinguished them from firms such as Gillette and Kodak in whose industries the product technology has evolved slowly over time. Table 11 lists the firms by product classification. Eastman Kodak produces amateur film, a branded consumer item that is also a "high technology" item. It has been placed in the latter category since we felt the technological aspects of the product were the predominant characteristics. The sample size, which has been limited to nine firms, is too small to permit development of a theory of the acquisition of dominance. It is large enough, however, to allow parallels in the histories of the firms to be observed which can provide a basis for future research.

The information presented in this and the following chapters is drawn from three sources. Industry studies, where available, provided the bulk of the material. They were supplemented by information from trade and business

Table 10.   Classification of Firms used in Case Studies by Age and Dominance

Old Dominant, Now Declined	Old Dominant, Currently Dominant	New Dominant
Coca-Cola	Campbell Soup	Boeing
Pullman, Inc.	Eastman Kodak	IBM
United Shoe (Emhart Corp.)	Gillette	Procter & Gamble

Table 11.   Classification of Firms used in Case Studies by Product Type

Branded Consumer Item	High Technology Item
Campbell Soup	Boeing
Coca-Cola	Eastman Kodak
Gillette	IBM
Procter & Gamble	Pullman, Inc.
	United Shoe

journals. Decisions and exhibits from major anti-trust cases were also reviewed.

Factors in the Original Creation of Dominance

In chapter 1 we reviewed several conditions which could facilitate the emergence of a dominant firm. Here we shall examine the histories of the sample firms to discover which factors appear most important in the creation of dominance. It is not the case that only one factor plays a role in the experience of each firm. Indeed, it may be that the conjunction of several are necessary for the development of a dominant firm and that if one alone was present, another market structure would have developed.

Innovation and Invention

Joseph Schumpeter observed that an important source of competition was "...the new commodity, the new technology, the new source of supply, the new type of organization."[1] Several of the firms in this sample exemplify Schumpeterian competition. Six out of nine of the firms invented the product around which an industry grew. Employees of Boeing, Kodak, and Campbell Soup either developed a new technology or adapted research done elsewhere to produce a radically new product. The companies of Gillette and Pullman were actually formed to exploit inventions, and Procter, although it did not actually develop detergents, performed research necessary to raise their cleaning effectiveness to such a level that they would be marketable. The remaining firms' innovations or inventions came in the areas of marketing or organizational form. Coca-Cola developed a new way of delivering a product, and United Shoe adopted an organizational form not previously used in the industry. IBM adapted the computer, which was invented by another firm, for use by a new class of customers.

Important as innovation may seem to an explanation of the acquisition of dominance, the new product and the new technology per se cannot explain the development of the dominant firm structure. Something must occur to prevent other firms from copying the innovation or invention. Dominance also depends upon factors that inhibit the arrival of Schumpeter's "swarm of imitators." Patents, for example, are a legal device to accomplish this. Alternatively, being first may allow the firm to benefit from economies of scale or learning effects. These latter factors are bases for dominance in their own right, and they will be examined later. They are mentioned here to emphasize that innovation alone does not imply a dominant firm structure will result.

Pullman developed a radical new means or technology of providing the service "rest" on trains. In a sense, it created the industry in which it became dominant. In 1858 George M. Pullman arranged with the Chicago & Alton Railroad to convert two of its day coaches into sleepers. These were not the first sleeping cars to have been built; they were, however, the first to embody Pullman's invention: an upper berth which could be closed in the day and which could also serve as a receptacle for bedding. Two important features of the Pullman cars which led to their acceptance were their increased safety, since they were heavier than sleepers constructed previously, and their luxury.[2]

King C. Gillette, a "Yankee inventor," set out to develop a product that people use every day and throw away, on the advice of a friend who had himself invented the crown cork bottle cap. He described his conception of the safety razor in somewhat romantic terms:

> I was living in Brookline (Mass.) at No. 2 Marion Terrace and I was consumed with the thought of inventing something that people would use and throw away and buy again. On one particular morning when I started to shave I found my razor dull, and it was not only dull but it was beyond the point of successful stropping and it needed honing, for which it must be taken to a barber or to a cutter. As I stood there with my razor in my hand, my eyes resting on it as lightly as a bird settling down on its nest—the Gillette razor was born. I saw it all in a moment, and in that same moment many unvoiced questions were asked and answered more with the rapidity of a dream than by the slow process of reasoning...[3]

Although the safety razor was conceived as early as 1895, six years were required before technical problems of production were solved. Many of these were handled by William E. Nickerson, another inventor. Gillette himself had a declining role in the commercial exploitation of the razor, and after 1930 he had neither legal nor effective control of the company.[4]

The remaining firms that invented the product in which they became dominant were already in existence and were producing in related areas. Kodak and Boeing made film and airplanes, although of different technologies. Campbell made tomato ketchup and canned vegetables while Procter & Gamble produced soap.

The Joseph Campbell Co. was established in 1869 as a canning business. As early as the 1890's, a time when most food companies employed "tasters," the company had the foresight to employ technically trained personnel. Dr. John T. Dorrance, one of its chemists, invented a means of condensing soup in 1897. The process involved quickly cooking fruit to avoid discoloration and mechanically removing a large portion of the acid-containing juice. The advantage of condensed soup was its reduced cost of transporation and storage.[5]

Synthetic detergents themselves were not invented by Procter & Gamble. The original detergents did not, however, clean cotton well. Procter's innovation was "building" detergents, that is, adding phosphates that facilitate cleaning by softening water and holding dirt in suspension.

Eastman Kodak is a good example of a firm whose original market power may be attributed to innovation. George Eastman was both an inventor and entrepreneur. Originally he was concerned with the technical aspects of the business and devoted his attention to simplifying the process of photography. The development of roll film and cameras by Kodak represented a radical change in the technology of photography; prior to this, the field was dominated by gelatin plates. When Eastman's roll film and cameras were not widely accepted by professional photographers, he turned to the general public as a market. It was upon this marketing innovation rather than inventions that his later success depended. Kodak cameras were aimed at the lowest common denominator consumer—one who knew nothing about taking pictures. Given that the public was the target of this marketing strategy, a choice had to be made about distribution channels. Eastman hit upon the idea of using drug stores. In an era of strict blue laws, they were the one place open on Sunday when most pictures were likely to be taken.[6] Although the invention itself was a necessary condition for Kodak's dominance, without Eastman's radical marketing innovation market power would not have been acquired.

Boeing is another firm that was able to use a change in technology to its advantage in establishing a dominant position. Up until 1958 Douglas remained the leader in the commercial aircraft field. Boeing, on the other hand, had suffered a series of disasters. It had lost about 50 million dollars in its attempt to modify the B-29 bomber for the commercial market. Management at Boeing decided to take the risks and pioneer the development of commercial jet aircraft—the alternative being to leave the commercial aircraft field entirely. They subsequently developed a prototype jet which could be used for both a commercial airplane and a military tanker. At the same time Douglas was occupied with meeting orders for the DC-6's and DC-7's and had no excess capacity with which to develop a jet. Boeing had test flown its prototype a year before Douglas began work on its jet, the DC-8. Although Douglas delivered its first DC-8 only six months after Boeing, it remained at a disadvantage. The prototype had allowed Boeing to sign up several airlines for early orders, and Boeing capitalized on its lead by quickly following the 707 with the 720 and 727.[7]

Not all of the firms in this sample necessarily developed a new product. Recall that Schumpeter also included new forms of organization in his typology of competition. United Shoe, IBM, and Coca-Cola brought new methods of distribution or organizational form to their industries rather than new products.

United Shoe Machinery Corporation was the result of a merger of several other companies. Its creation brought the big trust to its industry. Employing the trust as an organizational form was a departure from the way industry firms in the past had been organized and in this sense was an innovation.

Coca-Cola can be classified as an innovator in marketing; it was the first firm to develop a system of franchised bottlers. It must be noted, however, that this "innovation" was completely inadvertent on Coke's part. Asa Candler did not believe there was much demand for bottled soft drinks and sold Coke's bottling rights for one dollar to two lawyers from Chattanooga, Tennessee who had approached him about the idea. They developed the franchise system since they had insufficient capital to exploit the idea themselves.[8]

IBM did not rely on a technological invention or innovation for the acquisition of its dominance. Eckert and Mauchly, builders of the UNIVAC computer, approached IBM for funds to produce the machine commercially. Although scientists at IBM were enthusiastic, word came down from Watson that there was "no reasonable interaction possible between Eckert-Mauchly and IBM."[9] It was not until 1951 when the first UNIVAC was delivered to the Census Bureau that IBM recognized the threat computers posed to its punched card business.[10] IBM did innovate in its marketing methods. When it began producing computers it developed machines that could easily be used by its tabulating card customers. This marketing strategy played a role in its eventual acquisition of market power.

Invention and innovation play an important role in the process of acquiring dominance. In no case, however, is it the sole cause of dominance. Other firms attempted to copy the inventions of Pullman and Gillette. Synthetic detergents and roll film were produced by firms besides Procter & Gamble and Kodak. Douglas delivered a jet only six months behind Boeing. Being "first" is certainly important for a potentially dominant firm but this condition must be supported by other factors. We shall examine other conditions which themselves facilitate the development of a dominant firm structure or which combine with factors such as innovation to produce it.

Patents and Secrecy

Patents facilitate the acquisition of dominance by preventing the copying of inventions. Dominance acquired in this manner is legally protected. Firms may gain dominance as a result of patents without necessarily being an innovator if they buy them. Although acquiring patents through invention is of far more importance, one firm in this sample obtained a number of them through purchase.

Initially patents played a role in the experiences of all of the firms except Coca-Cola, IBM, and Boeing. The two latter firms are in areas in which technology is changing so rapidly that patents are of little use, and Coca-Cola has relied upon secrecy to protect its formula.

Patents are of more importance among the experiences of the old dominant firms. Both Pullman and United Shoe initially held several of them. In Pullman's case, they were important in the 1880's. Wagner Company, one of Pullman's competitors, found it impossible to build adequate sleeping cars without the use of Pullman patents. Pullman granted them licenses but only on cars run over certain rail lines. By 1940 no basic patents were in existence in the sleeping car industry.[11] Likewise, patents were more important at United Shoe's birth. By 1956, USMC's competitors admitted that any patents could be invented around, and patent protection had mostly expired on the twelve largest revenue earning machines.[12] Although both Pullman and United Shoe have since declined, their decrease in market power did not immediately follow patent expiration.

All of the old dominant firms that maintained their position held patents on their products. Campbell Soup Company was issued the patent for Dr. Dorrance's process of treating fruits in 1913. It thus had a protected position until 1930. Gillette enjoyed a protected patent position until 1921, and during that time it did not license to other manufacturers. George Eastman used patents as a means of limiting entry and establishing a "natural monopoly." He did not rely solely on production patents but sought to develop systems of patents covering both process and product. The strategy worked well in the case of roll holders, roll film, and roll-film cameras. Even if the patents were neither important nor strong, they were not allowed to lapse. Reese V. Jenkins in *Images and Enterprise: Technology and the American Photographic Industry 1839 to 1925* cites office correspondence between George Eastman and Eastman Photo Materials Co. in which Eastman notes that the greatest profits are to be found in film manufacture and requests that patents on its manufacture be maintained, regardless of their strength, for their potential effect on the morale of competitors.[13] In the effort to cover every avenue, Eastman also purchased firms in order to acquire their patents.[14]

The only new dominant firm for which patents played a role was Procter & Gamble. From 1949 until 1966, Tide's high-phosphate formula was protected by one of the detergent industry's rare patents. In early years, Procter did not issue licenses.[15]

Economies of Scale/Learning Effects

Economies of scale that permit a producer with a higher rate of production to manufacture at lower average cost than a producer with a lower rate are one common explanation of the market power of dominant firms. This is, however, an essentially static explanation of the existence of a non-competitive market structure. It does not suggest why one firm became dominant, nor does it explain the continued existence of the fringe firms. If lower costs are associated with indivisible capital equipment, for example, then the dominant firm may have been the first firm that was able to acquire it. If demand is insufficient, other firms will not find it profitable to acquire the same piece of equipment. Economies may be more important in explaining the persistence of a dominant firm structure than in explaining the acquisition of dominance. If they play a role in the acquisition of market power they must be combined with other factors that allow them to be realized by one firm before others.

Alternatively, costs may be related to cumulative volume of output. A decline in costs over time as workers become more proficient and the best methods of production are developed is known as "learning effects." Learning effects may be either firm specific or industry specific. A decline in costs as workers become more skillful is firm specific, but costs may also decrease for the industry as firms refine the techniques of production. While the dominant firm may have been able to accumlate experience by being the first to lower its costs, in the latter case being first might not necessarily be an advantage. Firms could enter later with lower costs. As an explanation of the sources of dominance, we expect the former firm specific effects to be more important although industry effects suggest dominance may be obtained by late entrants who are good copiers.

Evidence related to economies of scale is difficult to obtain. For three firms, previous case studies provided estimates of the importance of scale economies. The evidence for the remaining firms was drawn from firm or industry reports and is necessarily more casual. IBM and Boeing were two of the firms on which extensive studies had been done, and their case for economies or learning effects is strongest. The other firm, United Shoe, did not appear to owe much of its market power to either source. For the remaining firms, casual evidence indicates that Pullman and Kodak may have realized some economies.

IBM is the best instance of a firm that owes some of its market power to scale economies. The data processing industry is characterized by distinct segments, and the importance of economies differs in each of them: central processing units (CPU's), peripherals, software, maintenance, and marketing. In the production of CPU's, economies of scale are most pronounced. An exhibit presented in the *Telex vs. IBM* case provides evidence of the expected cost for producing various quantities of the 370/168 CPU. If the entire market were 1,000 machines, a competitor with a 50% market share would have 5.8% higher costs than one with a 100% market share. A competitor with a 10% market share would have 43.8% higher costs. Part of these economies are related to high fixed costs incurred in training production workers and experimenting in production methods rather than indivisible capital equipment. Gerald Brock, in his study of the computer industry, also suggests that costs fall over time as a result of the learning process, although he makes no quantitative estimate of learning effects.[16]

In the manufacture of peripheral computation equipment, economies appear to be small. On the IBM 2401-5 tape drive, as much as 46% of the costs were from purchased components, and an IBM study concluded that it had only a 15% cost advantage in circuits due to its own production. A company with 10% of IBM's market share would incur approximately 10% higher costs per unit.

In the areas of software, maintenance, and promotion, economies may be significant. The randomness of breakdowns and travel time generate economies in maintenance. Brock estimated the following cost disadvantages in maintenance relative to a firm with 100% of the market: 6% higher costs for a firm with a 25% market share, and 15 to 20% higher costs with a 9% market share. Because marketing is done largely by salesmen, economies also arise as a result of travel costs in that stage of production. They are of importance in software to the extent that utility programs, language compilers, and system control programs are transferable among customers.[17]

The aircraft industry, like the computer industry, faces large fixed costs related to the development of a new generation of aircraft. The resulting cost structure is one in which initial costs are high but average total cost falls rapidly as the fixed costs are spread over increasing units of output. The nature of the production process in the industry is such that as a cumulative volume of output rises, costs fall as workers learn their jobs and the best methods of production are discovered. The learning effects alone are estimated to give a 20% decrease in unit costs for each doubling of output.[18]

The production of shoe machinery like the production of computers is composed of a number of "stages" at which economies of scale could arise. Carl Kaysen in *United States vs. United Shoe Machinery Corporation* uses the evidence presented in that case to estimate economies at various points in the production process. In the manufacturing stage, economies are primarily the result of the "borrowing" of parts among machines. A long product line would thus be most conducive to scale economies. The proportion of parts which may be borrowed ranges from 2% to 8% on the various machines. Since these parts are standardized and can be readily purchased, no economies arise in their manufacture. Kaysen also concludes that service could be provided with branch offices having approximately 27 personnel which a firm of one-half United Shoe's size could handle. This implies the service bureau of USMC did not reflect economies either. Likewise, Kaysen concluded there was no evidence of economies in distribution. The work was not specialized, and personnel and office space could be varied with the work load.[19]

The evidence related to economies of scale for the remaining firms is more casual. Pullman's policy in the construction of sleeping cars was to make them on a few uniform designs in order to reap economies in the servicing as well as manufacturing of the cars, but standard sources reveal no estimates of their quantitative importance.[20]

In the case of Campbell Soup there is suggestive evidence that economies of scale are not an explanation for its acquisition of market power. The plants themselves are located in agricultural regions in which the raw materials are produced. The potential labor force in an area limits their size.[21] Individual batches of soup vary from 115 to 600 gallons. The more ingredients in a soup, the smaller the batch in which it must be made. At crucial stages of the production process, such as doling the proper number of oysters into a can, humans out-perform machines.[22] These facts do not suggest large economies of scale at the plant level.

In the 1880's, George Eastman established a sole distributor relationship with one of the nation's strongest photographic jobbers. As a result, he was able to achieve economies of scale in the production of gelatin plates.[23] That was the major photographic medium which preceded roll film. As such, it only indirectly contributed to Kodak's dominance.

Procter & Gamble has the potential for economies of scale either at the production stage or the distribution stage. The basic ingredient of a synthetic detergent is a surface-active agent or surfactant that constitutes 15 to 20% of the formula and is chiefly responsible for soil removal.[24] The manufacture of a surfactant is in two steps: preparation of the alkylate which is ordinarily carried out by chemical firms, and sulphonation or neutralization, which is ordinarily done by the soap processor. This second step is adaptable to small-scale production so no economies of scale arise there.[25] Some economies of scale arise in Procter & Gamble's distribution process. As early as 1920 they began direct selling to retailers through a national sales force. One salesperson sells an entire product line which is quite long.[26] For a firm with its own sales force approximately 3% of net sales are allocated to selling expenses, but if a firm sells through food brokers this figure may be as high as 12 to 13%.[27]

The production of syrup itself is only a small part of the job of Coca-Cola, which must also provide technical assistance to bottlers and plan promotions. Scale economies are likely to arise in these latter activities but are probably not substantial. There do not appear to be any economies in the production of syrup itself.

Although economies of scale receive a large emphasis in the theoretical literature, they played a minor role in the acquisition of dominance by this sample of firms. IBM and Boeing experienced economies in production, and Procter & Gamble experienced them in distribution. There was casual evidence that Pullman realized them in manufacturing and servicing. Boeing was the first to produce jet aircraft, and it was able to garner large initial orders. The resulting economies of scale and learning effects from those large orders helped it to acquire a dominant market position. Procter's economies in distribution arise from the fact that it has a long line of products over which to spread selling costs. The sales network was already in existence when Procter began producing detergents, so it was immediately able to realize lower costs in this area. Procter's economies were not dependent upon being first. The remaining firm, IBM, was not first but still was able to realize economies of scale. Other firms could not fully achieve them prior to its entrance, for although not an inventor or innovator, IBM proved to be a quick follower.

Natural Advantage

Possession of a vital input or control of a unique location can lead to market power. However, in the experiences of the firms which are part of our sample, natural advantages do not play a role in the origin of market power. Strategic location of plants is important for Campbell Soup which must locate its plants in agricultural areas close to raw materials and a water supply that meets certain quality specifications. In general, attempts are made to locate in areas with at least two railroads and a major truck highway.[28] Regardless of these criteria it is unlikely that Campbell controls all such locations in the United States.

Considering inputs to the production process of the firms, both Coca-Cola's and Campbell Soup's main inputs are agricultural products, and they do not have exclusive control over them. For both the production of razor blades and detergents a number of suppliers of raw materials are available. In the case of detergents, over forty companies supply materials although some specialize in only a small area.[29]

One input of importance in both the production of computers and commercial airplanes is a technically trained labor supply, but manpower has been mobile among the firms in these industries. Douglas, the firm which initially was dominant in commercial aircraft, benefited from an association with the California Institute of Technology. However, when Boeing realized its disadvantage in aerodynamics, it was able to build an excellent engineering group in that field.[30] Personnel have readily switched from established to new firms in the computer industry, too.[31] Thus, neither Boeing nor IBM owes its market power to control of labor inputs.

In 1898 Eastman Kodak and American Aristotype negotiated exclusive agency status with General Paper Company for raw paper used in producing photographic paper. For almost forty years the mills owned by General Paper had produced the world's entire stock of raw photographic paper. Paper used in photography must be free of minerals to be suitable for coating, and these mills were located in areas where the water was virtually mineral free. Kodak and American Aristotype used the agreement to force price maintenance on dealers and coaters. Dealers received discounts for complying with list prices, and coaters were not sold paper until they agreed to certain terms of sale. The agreement also contained the proviso that companies not participating would be purchased as soon as they could be obtained at a reasonable price. This strategy was not successful in limiting domestic competition in photographic paper as companies developed new kinds of raw paper stock. Indeed, it placed Eastman at a disadvantage since the agreements prohibited them from purchasing paper from any other source and from experimenting with new paper. Although for a time Eastman had control of a unique input, it did not ensure market domination. Because of the manner in which Eastman set out to control the raw paper stock, its behvior may be described as predatory or exclusionary. This will be examined as a factor in the acquisition of dominance in a later section.[32]

Mergers and Acquisitions

Mergers may be either horizontal, vertical, or conglomerate and may affect market structure in a variety of ways. While horizontal mergers function by absorbing competitors, vertical integration can result in dominance through (a) cutting off competitors from a resource or channel of distribution, a form of predation; (b) increases in quality control of the firm through control of inputs; (c) lower costs of the firm; (d) allowing the firm to capture all of the benefits of innovations through keeping of trade secrets; (e) decreasing "bottlenecks" in various stages of the production. Conglomerate mergers between firms operating in separate and distinct markets will be discussed in chapter 5.

Mergers are of more importance as a source of dominance in the experiences of the older dominant firms. United Shoe Machinery, Eastman Kodak, and Pullman were all participants in a number of mergers or acquisitions. Among the newer dominant firms, IBM and Procter & Gamble established their market power following changes in technology, but both firms had substantial market power prior to the technical change in which mergers played a role. We shall examine these early mergers since capital created then was later employed in the acquisition of dominance in the "new" product areas.

United Shoe Machinery Corporation was formed on February 7, 1889 as a consolidation of Goodyear Shoe Machinery Corporation, Consolidated and McKay Lasting Machine Company, Eppler Welt Machine Company, and Davey Pegging Machine Company. Goodyear, Consolidated and McKay Lasting, and McKay Shoe Machinery each produced different types of machines and were dominant in their respective branches of the industry. Table 12 gives the market share in various machines of the constituent companies. Later growth also involved a series of acquisitions of businesses, patents, and inventions. From 1899 to 1911 United Shoe concluded 59 acquisitions of one sort or another, and between 1916 and 1937 it concluded a series of 27 acquisitions. Table 13 gives the number of acquisitions per year and the acquisitions by type. Not all of these mergers or acquisitions were major. The most important ones were the acquisition in 1910 of the Thomas G. Plant Shoe Company which claimed to have a complete line of machinery and the acquisition of competitors with products superior to United: A.E. Little and Henne-Pro.[33]

Eastman Kodak displays a similar experience. Between 1895 and 1909 it purchased three firms in roll film as part of its patent protection policy. To obtain a full line of products it entered the plate camera market by purchasing four companies that made either cameras or parts, including Century Camera Company, the most successful plate company.[34] Kodak also integrated forward into distribution between 1902 and 1915 by purchasing sixteen houses that sold photographic supplies.[35] Each time Kodak entered a new part of the industry through acquisition, it sought both a large market share and patents. A side effect of these acquisitions was that Kodak also acquired the services of a number of key technical personnel.[36]

Between 1867 and 1900 the Pullman Company had acquired every other sleeping car concern in the United States. The last acquisition was the Wagner Palace Car Company which had also absorbed other companies. In the case of Wagner, the initial overtures for acquisition were made by the seller.[37] Pullman was not left without competitors. American Car and Foundry was established in the same year that Pullman merged with Wagner. In addition, railroad shops built some of their own cars.

Mergers have not played a major role as a source of dominance in the experiences of the remaining "old" dominant firms—Coca-Cola, Campbell Soup, and Gillette—although Gillette did acquire the assets of Autostrop Safety Razor Co., Inc., in 1930. A series of related product acquisitions were more important, and these will be discussed later.

For the new dominant firms, mergers played no role in the acquisition of dominance itself. However, the firms were involved in acquisitions earlier in their histories in which they gained resources of use later.

Table 12.   Market Share in Various Machines of the Constituent
Companies of United Shoe*

Goodyear Shoe Machinery Corporation	60% welt inseamers and sewers 10% lasters
Consolidated and McKay Lasting Machine Company	60% lasters
McKay Shoe Machinery Company	70% healing 80% other metallic fastening
Davey Pegging Machine Company	7% pegging machines
Eppler Welt Machine Company	10% inseaming and welt sewing

* Source: Reprinted by permission of the publishers from *United States vs. United Shoe Machinery Corporation: An Economic Analysis of an Anti-Trust Case,* by Carl Kaysen. Cambridge, Mass.: Harvard University Press. Copyright © 1956 by the President and Fellows of Harvard College, pp. 6-7.

Table 13.   Acquisitions of United Shoe: Number per Year and Type*

Acquisitions per Year 1899-1911		Acquisitions 1899-1911	Acquisitions 1916-1937
1899	11	20 New machines not previously	2 Acquisitions of inventor's
1900	8	made by United	services
1901	6	11 Improved machines	3 Acquisitions of services and
1902	6	15 Finding and supplies businesses	patents without a going business
1903	3	3 Contracts of employment with	11 Acquisitions of patents without
1904	9	inventions	a going business
1905	1	3 Patent acquisitions	11 Acquisitions of patents with
1906	3	3 Patent acquisitions to settle	a going business
1907	1	litigation	
1908	3	2 Employment contracts arising out	
1909	1	of transactions of constituent	
1910	6	companies	
1911	1	1 Exclusive license under patent	
		on supplies	

* Source: Reprinted by permission of the publishers from *United States vs. United Shoe Machinery Corporation: An Economic Analysis of an Anti-Trust Case,* by Carl Kaysen. Cambridge, Mass.: Harvard University Press. Copyright © 1956 by the President and Fellows of Harvard College, pp. 6-8, 59-61.

IBM was incorporated as Computing-Tabulating-Recording Co. in 1911, the result of a merger of three companies. Between 1911 and 1924 the company was involved in two additional acquisitions before it merged with International Business Machines Corp. and assumed that name. Since then the company has acquired a number of assets or businesses in the fields of counting or weighing machines, typewriters, scales, and postal meters.[38] When the change in technology from tabulating to computing occurred, IBM built machines that appealed to its established base of customers. The loyalty of these customers helped it acquire dominance in computers.[39]

Like IBM, Procter & Gamble participated in a number of acquisitions prior to its dominance in synthetic detergents. Between 1929 and 1945 Procter was involved in eight major acquisitions: three businesses which produced raw materials for soap production, three soap producers, and two not specified.[40] It has also participated in a series of product extension mergers to be discussed later. The sales network which Procter retained from soap products was a factor in its later dominance in detergents as well as its long line of products over which sales costs could be spread.

The majority of vertical integration by dominant firms has been accomplished through an expansion of production facilities within the firm itself rather than through mergers. It will thus be discussed in those chapters concerning the behavior of dominant firms.

The most interesting case of vertical integration through merger was Boeing, which was engaged not only in the production of aircraft but also in their operation. The original properties of Boeing Airplane Company were part of the holding company of aeronautical concerns known as United Aircraft & Transport Corporation. The Air Mail Act of 1934 required companies competing for air mail contracts to be separate from airplane manufacturing companies. As a result, Boeing Airplane Company and Boeing Air Transport, the predecessor of United Airlines, were divested, but prior to that the transport operation purchased planes from Boeing. Even after the act there continued to be some joint development of aircraft by manufacturers and airlines. The Boeing 247 was initially used exclusively by United and the DC-2 by TWA which had been associated with Douglas.[41]

Mergers thus played a small role overall in the acquisition of dominance. Even among the old dominant firms, they were of importance only in the cases of United Shoe and Pullman. Kodak and Gillette acquired companies but this was incidental to their acquisition of market power. Mergers which could create a dominant firm are now proscribed by anti-trust statutes, thus they are not important in the experiences of the new firms.

Product Loyalty

If consumers display a preference for the goods of one firm over others, assuming for the moment that prices are equal, then we may say that the first firm has been able to generate product loyalty. It is possible that the attributes of all the firms' products are the same and that this is known to consumers, in which case they prefer the product of the one firm simply for its image. More likely is the case in which the preferred product has different attributes such as better quality control, a higher degree of standardization, or better service facilities. All of the products produced by this sample of firms are differentiated to some extent. It may therefore be that product differentiation is a necessary but not sufficient condition for dominance.

Product loyalty may, of course, be the result rather than the cause of dominance. For example, customers may believe that a firm as large as IBM or Campbell Soup will "stand behind its product" and buy it for that reason. Here we are concerned only with product loyalty as a source of dominance, and we shall delay discussion of the reverse possibility until a later chapter.

A symptom of the product loyalty which many dominant firms have generated is the fact that their product is identified with the industry itself. "Pullman" became at one point in time a synonym for a sleeping car, and "Coke" is often used as a generic term for a soft drink. In an investigation of the acquisition of dominance, the important question is how the products of these firms came to be so closely associated with their industries' products.

Two important factors in the acceptance of Pullman cars were their increased safety due to heavier construction and their luxury. Although not the first sleeping cars, Pullman cars redefined the concept. Other firms were required to meet their standards of safety and comfort.[42]

The product loyalty which Coca-Cola generated was primarily based upon its taste—the factor upon which a soft drink's success ultimately depends. Coke has always jealously guarded its formula and has gone to great lengths to maintain the differences between its product and that of other soft drink companies. Advertising is one device it used to reinforce these differences. Asa Candler, the first head of the Coca-Cola Company, recognized the value of advertising, and it played an important role even when Coca-Cola was young. One of the earlier promotion methods involved the distribution and redemption of complimentary tickets entitling the holder to a free glass of Coca-Cola. As an inducement to get druggists and other dispensers to carry Coke, they were promised free tickets to hand out to their customers. In addition to developing a consumer preference for Coca-Cola's "unique" taste, when Candler took over its manufacture, he also made changes in the production facilities to improve the stability of the drink and to assure that it was of uniform quality.[43]

Just as the products of Coca-Cola and Pullman became identified with their industries, Eastman Kodak has become synonymous with film. George Eastman established quality as a competitive strategy early in the company's history. Testifying in Kodak's defense in a 1915 anti-trust case, he attributed its market power to a product of consistently good quality:

> ... It is not that anybody cannot make the same kind of film, but it is making film exactly the same everyday, and the man that can do it must get the trade, because there is so much dependent upon it.[44]

In his testimony, Eastman recognized another point of importance in considering the effect of product loyalty on a firm's market power. Consumers evaluate the loss they will suffer if a product "fails" in some sense. If the consequences of loss are great, quality becomes of importance in their evaluation of a product and will even more likely be a factor contributing to dominance. In the case of photographic film, a picture lost is gone forever, and consumers will rate product quality heavily.

The essence of product loyalty is that consumers believe one product has "attributes" which others do not have. Coca-Cola emphasized its unique taste, Pullman its luxury, and Kodak its uniform quality. Procter & Gamble also relies heavily upon unique product attributes to produce product loyalty. The introduction of Cheer by Procter & Gamble is a good case study of an attempt to generate product loyalty in the detergent industry. In 1950, four years after the introduction of Tide, Procter decided to launch a new detergent. An alternative strategy to introducing a new brand is to introduce a different "facing" or size of an old product. This was rejected since there already were three sizes of Tide, and it would not reach consumers who did not like Tide. Cheer was introduced and was considered by Procter to perform better than Tide under certain conditions. Initially it did not sell well. Blue coloring matter was added to Cheer in addition to the optical bleach which it already contained, and it was advertised as imparting "blue whiteness." By 1953 Cheer was the second largest selling detergent behind Tide. Although it was similar to other detergents, it looked different and that was its selling point.[45]

A technique of generating product loyalty not available to firms producing branded consumer products is to develop and maintain close ties with the customers. Business practices which may accomplish this include providing service and consulting help as well as leasing. Both United Shoe and IBM employed these competitive strategies.

Close contact between shoe manufacturers and United was sustained through a lease-only policy, and service was incidental to the lease. In addition, United offered a full line of machines which supported its market power through extra selling effectiveness. United could thus present itself as a firm able to meet all of the shoe manufacturer's needs.[46]

IBM has employed these tactics in its generation of product loyalty. The nature of its product makes close ties between producer and consumer even more likely. Customers have trouble evaluating computers or computer services. The performance of machines is difficult to measure, and buyers show wide disagreement about what factors are of importance in their selection. IBM sales personnel emphasize the customer applications rather than the hardware. This establishes the idea that the product "sold" is not the computer but rather the services which flow from the machine. Customers become used to a firm which "solves their computing problems" and associate this with a product quality difference. The practice of selling systems further increases the difficulty of product choice since components are not evaluated on their own merit. In addition, IBM has tied software and hardware into a product package with one price.[47] Besides distinguishing itself from companies which operate at only one stage of the production process, this systems approach focuses competition on the company itself and its total package of services rather than the product. Because the cost of product failure is high for users of computers, they are also susceptible to the generation of product loyalty through the provision of consulting help and service.

As a factor in the acquisition of dominance, "product loyalty" is a rubric for a host of reasons why consumers prefer the product of one firm to that of others. The products may have different attributes as in the cases of Pullman and Kodak, or the "loyalty" may result from business practices as in the cases of United Shoe and IBM. Alternatively, it may be based upon consumers' taste preferences or product "attributes" with no function. Such were the experiences of Coca-Cola and Procter & Gamble. For an analysis of the acquisition of dominance the "reason" for the development of product loyalty makes little difference, however, from a policy standpoint it will make a great deal of difference. Loyalty based upon business practices or imagined product differences has different welfare implications than that based upon quality differences.

Predation

One way to achieve market power is through the failure of competitors as a result of predatory or exclusionary activity. The classic example of predation is cutting price below marginal cost to drive competitors out of business. It also includes behavior which deprives competitors of a vital input, supplies, or a marketing channel. Exclusionary behavior can be broadly defined. Judge Hand suggested that to progressively embrace opportunities and to face newcomers with capacity was exclusionary. Various marketing devices, such as leasing, or systems introductions of products, may also fall into this category.

There is no evidence among this sample of firms of the use of price as a predatory device to acquire dominance. Instead, the firms employed various exclusive dealing arrangements or acquired patents to prevent them from being available to competitors.

Eastman Kodak, along with American Aristotype, sought to "rationalize" the photographic paper industry through agreements which gave them exclusive agency status for raw paper stock. In addition, they were provided with discounts for production of fighting brands, that is, low-priced papers used to undersell competitors. In return for the above agreement, Kodak promised not to experiment in developing other sources of raw paper. Control of the raw paper stock was not a major source of Kodak's long-run dominance. Competitors were able to develop new sources of raw paper, and Kodak itself was relegated to the role of follower rather than innovator.[48]

United Shoe also exhibited some exclusionary behavior. It tried to prevent a Henne-Pro machine from coming to market via patent infringement suits and when this failed the machine was purchased. In his study of United Shoe, Kaysen found eight examples of acquisitions for their "hedging" value and three examples of acquisitions for "fencing" purposes. Patents for hedging purposes were acquired on devices which were the second-best alternative to a United machine; patents for fencing purposes were acquired because they might be useful to a competitor. Finally, there is evidence that United enforced lease clauses differentially depending upon the amount of competition it faced in a particular machine type. [49]

The marketing arrangement between the Pullman Company and Pullman-Standard may be interpreted as exclusionary. Prior to 1927 Pullman both manufactured and operated sleeping cars. In that year two units, the Pullman Company and Pullman Car and Manufacturing Company (later renamed Pullman-Standard Car and Manufacturing Company), were created from the original firm and organized as a holding company. The reorganization was a result of the Clayton Act which placed limits on purchases among firms with interlocking directors. Pullman Standard supplied sleeping cars to the Pullman Company which operated them. Railroads could either contract with the Pullman Company for the provision of sleeping car service, or they could operate their own cars. Prior to the Department of Justice anti-trust suit against Pullman in 1940, the Pullman Company refused to operate cars not built by Pullman-Standard. The relationship between Pullman and Pullman-Standard contributed to the dominance of Pullman-Standard in sleeping cars. Railroads found it easier and more convenient to contract with the Pullman Company for the provision of their sleeping car service. While in 1899 there were twenty railroads operating their own service, by 1936 seventeen of these had contracts with Pullman for full service and the remaining three had contracts for partial service. [50] The net effect was to exclude other car builders since they could only sell to railroads which were willing to operate sleeping cars themselves. Over time, this represented a dwindling number of railroads.

Predation or exclusionary activity is not a major source of market power for this sample of firms. United Shoe's patent acquisitions and Kodak's raw paper agreements played minor roles in the development of a dominant firm structure. Pullman Company's refusal to operate non-Pullman-Standard cars is of more importance. The provision of sleeping car service has dimensions of a natural monopoly while the construction of the cars does not. The refusal to operate non-Pullman cars enabled market power in the service of cars to be transferred to the industry for their construction. It must, however, be remembered that the Pullman Company and Pullman-Standard were once one company; they organized in holding company form as a result of the Clayton Act. Their agreement merely continued a practice of "exclusive" dealing begun earlier. In one sense the source of dominance is not exclusion but the natural monopoly aspects of sleeping car service. Nevertheless, given that the companies were separate, the agreements prevented other firms from competing.

Historic Accident

The idea that market power might in some sense be accidental was advanced by Learned Hand in the *United States vs. Alcoa* decision. In the sample of firms examined here we have found no evidence of sudden changes in tastes or costs, for example, leading to dominance.

Superior Skill or Business Acumen

Market power is often attributed to the "superior skill" of the firm holding it. The term originates in the legal literature dealing with monopolization and is used as a catchall for market power obtained not by restraint of trade but by the particular foresight of one firm. It has no particular definition but is interpreted in the context of individual cases. Innovation and invention which are included here separately are considered evidence of superior skill in anti-trust cases. For example, under George Eastman's leadership, Kodak developed roll cameras and film as well as a strategy for marketing them. Likewise, management at Boeing displayed unusual ability in their decision to develop a plane involving a new technology.

The concept of "superior skill" is not limited simply to inventions, but includes organizational innovations as well. Procter & Gamble's development of a marketing organization, known as the brand manager system, is another example of superior skill. Neil McElroy, a member of Procter's advertising department in the 1930's, came up with the idea of separate brand manager teams for individual products.[51] This system made possible Procter's strategy of multiple entries in product categories and is now common practice among large consumer product firms.

Little can be said about the importance of "skill" in the acquisition of dominance; the category itself is only loosely defined. It does indicate that the creation of market power generally involves a number of different factors which sometimes may be hard to classify and are simply evidence of the unusual insight of a firm or its leader.

Summary and Conclusions

Summary of Sources of Dominance

This survey has pointed out a number of factors which played a role in the acquisition of market power by a group of dominant firms. The sample of firms is so small that it is not possible to develop a rigorous theory of the acquisition of dominance. Several common themes were observed, however, and these are summarized in table 14.

Table 14. Factors in the Acquisition of Dominance

United Shoe	Innovation (Organizational)			Merger	Loyalty
Pullman	Invention	Patents	Economies (Production & Service)	Merger	Loyalty
Coca-Cola	Innovation (Marketing)				Loyalty
Eastman Kodak	Invention	Patents			Loyalty
Gillette	Invention	Patents			Loyalty
Campbell Soup	Invention	Patents			Loyalty
IBM	Innovation (Marketing)		Economies (Production)		Loyalty
Boeing	Invention		Economies (Production)		Loyalty
Procter & Gamble	Invention and Innovation (Marketing)	Patents	Economies (Distribution)		Loyalty

One of the most important results of this survey is that no firm owed its market power to only one factor or "source" of dominance. Dominance is the result of two or more factors which reinforce and support each other. Even United Shoe, which owed part of its market power to a merger, also relied on product loyalty generated through its leasing policy and the trust as an organizational innovation. Mergers played a role in Pullman's acquisition of dominance, but they occurred simultaneously with invention and patent protection. At least one of the acquired firms approached Pullman because it was having difficulty competing without access to the Pullman patents. Kodak, Gillette, and Campbell also invented their products, but patents were required to prevent imitators. In addition, they were able to generate product loyalty as a result of the quality of their products, advertising, and dealerships. Coca-Cola followed a similar pattern. Although it did not invent the soft drink, it was associated with the development of franchised bottlers, a marketing innovation. Its formula was protected by secrecy rather than patents. Procter & Gamble is interesting for the large number of factors which played a role in its dominance. It invented its product and held patents on it, but it also invested in product loyalty. Finally, because Procter markets a large number of products, it experienced economies of scale in distribution. The brand manager system allowed multiple entries in single product categories. The remaining two firms,

Boeing and IBM, owe part of their market power to economies of scale. IBM combined this with product loyalty, part of which was carried over from its tabulating card business and part of which resulted from close manufacturer-customer ties. Boeing's dominance was a result of its innovation as well as the economies of scale it has realized in production.

The various factors which interact to create dominance may be classified as "active" or "passive." Active sources require that the firm take some competitive move: they include invention or innovation, merger, product loyalty, and predation. Passive sources, on the other hand, are outside the control of the firms. They may be technologically or legally grounded. Examples of passive sources of market power include economies of scale, natural advantages, patents, and historic accident. The examination of the experiences of this sample of firms revealed no instance of a firm which owed its market power solely to passive factors. United Shoe's and Coca-Cola's positions were entirely the result of active factors, and the remaining firms relied on a combination of active and passive factors. Market power did not come unbidden to these firms, however, the fact that they played an active role in its creation does not necessarily condemn it. Invention or innovation is an "active" source of dominance and played a role in the creation of market power for all firms. This is a characteristic of good market performance. The second most frequently cited factor in the creation of dominance was product loyalty. This was a rubric for a number of different activities. Some product loyalty resulted from high quality products and other from business practices. While the former is desirable, the latter should be judged on a case-by-case basis.

Variation in the Factors Creating Dominance Over Time

The sample of firms was chosen so that it contained a mixture of firms which acquired their dominance in the early decades of the twentieth century and firms whose dominance dates from the post-World War II era. This allows us to gain insights into possible changes in the sources of dominance with time.

As we hypothesized earlier, mergers were important only in the experiences of the old firms; anti-trust activity has sharply circumscribed their role in the acquisition of dominance. In their place, economies of scale have taken on new importance. They were a factor in the creation of market power for all of the "new" dominant firms. The increased importance of economies of scale may be the result of general technical change which has raised the minimum optimal scale of production in all industries. Alternatively, anti-trust activity may have constrained the development of market power due to other factors such that only growth due to economies of scale, a defensible source of market power, remains.

Among the remaining factors which played a role in the histories of this sample of firms, innovation and product loyalty continue to be important.

Among the new dominant firms, only Procter & Gamble relied on patents. This is the result of the relatively higher rate of technical change in the new firms than the old rather than time itself.

Anti-trust activity has had some effect on the development of market power over time. Certainly it has closed off the quick route of the merger. Current development of dominant firms tends to be based upon a combination of invention, economies of scale, and product loyalty. This new dominance may prove to be more durable or persistent than the old dominance, but a judgment in this area must wait until the behavior of the sample of firms is examined in later chapters.

The Effect of Product Type on the Acquisition of Dominance

A product type classification proved helpful in understanding the behavior of dominant firms in the statistical studies above. Here we shall examine whether the factors which generate market power are in any way a function of product type. Because of the small sample size, the results can only be considered tentative.

Inventions and innovation seem to be of equal importance for firms producing high technology products and for firms producing branded consumer products. But innovation alone does not generate market power. All but one of the firms making branded consumer items supplemented invention or innovation with patent protection. The firm which did not hold a patent, Coca-Cola, employed secrecy instead. Only two out of five of the producers of high technology items held patents; this is primarily the result of the speed of technical change in these industries which negates the usefulness of patents. High technology firms rely more on economies of scale. There was at least casual evidence of economies in the cases of three out of five high technology firms but only one of four branded consumer products firms.

Product loyalty played an important role in the acquisition of dominance for firms producing both product types. However, it was generated in a number of different ways. Firms producing branded consumer products generate loyalty through quality differences, such as Campbell Soup and Gillette, and through differences in products which consumers perceive, such as Coca-Cola and Procter & Gamble. Loyalty as a result of activities which create ties between the producer and consumer is limited to firms making producer goods—IBM and United Shoe. Because Kodak makes a consumer product it cannot easily employ these tactics, although it has a network of dealers that functions somewhat in that manner. In general, its product loyalty is based upon quality.

The factors which are important for the creation of market power are not unique to each product type. Invention and innovation play a part for both. What does differ is the factors which supplement innovation. Producers of branded consumer products rely on patents and product loyalty. High technology firms often realize economies of scale, and to the extent that product loyalty plays a role, it is more often a function of manufacturer-customer ties.

Not all of the factors tending to create dominance are generated with equal ease. Product loyalty may be obtained only after a certain period of time has elapsed, and learning effects are by definition dependent upon the cumulative volume of output. Patents, on the other hand, only require approval of the patent application. To the extent that the factors which create market power differ systematically by product type, so will the ease of creating dominance. We hypothesized above that product type would affect the ease of both establishing and maintaining dominance. More specifically, we hypothesized that technology-intensive goods were subject to frequent change which gave rise both to easy initial dominance and to difficult maintenance of dominance. Conversely, consumer items were more likely to owe their dominance to product loyalty which was not subject to rapid erosion; it would thus be more difficult to establish but more durable.

Innovation was certainly of importance in establishing the dominance of Kodak, Boeing, and IBM. Kodak's roll film system of photography was a major change from the gelatin dry plates which were then the prevailing technology. IBM and Boeing both established dominance in fields following a major technological change. IBM maintained a position which it held from a related product industry while Boeing was able to supplant the previous leader.

After the technological switch from tabulators to computers, IBM developed a product which appealed to its current base of customers; the IBM 650 was "sold" as a device which could read punched cards rapidly and was a tabulating machine. IBM quickly capitalized upon the success of the 650 by introducing a number of models which were technically superior to those of Univac. These early computers were based upon vacuum tubes. The switch to transistors in the second generation of computers reveals how technical change makes the maintenance of dominance difficult. The transistor was developed independently of the data processing industry at Bell Telephone Laboratories in 1948. By the mid-1950's, prices had been reduced dramatically, and it had become competitive with vacuum tubes. Univac, declining because of an inferior product line, introduced a transistorized computer in August of 1958 at the same time that IBM delivered its business-oriented vacuum tube machine, the 7090. This technological switch brought the last group of entrants into the industry. Philco, already a producer of transistors, integrated forward. RCA, GE, and Autonetics also entered the market with transistor computers. In all, five companies preceded IBM which did not deliver its transistorized 7090 until the end of 1959. During this period, IBM's market power declined, but competitors were not able to make large in-roads due to a lack of marketing and production facilities. Figure 1 shows the trend in IBM's market share of computer installations.

Figure 1. Market Concentration in Computer Installations*

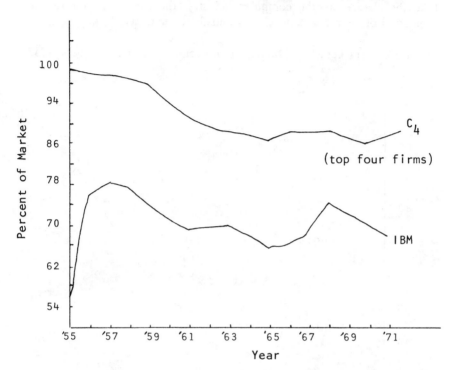

* Source: 1955-1967 figures from *Honeywell vs. Sperry Rand Decision,* p. 157. 1968-1971 figures from *Computers and Automation* censuses. Reprinted with permission from Gerald W. Brock. *The U.S. Computer Industry: A Study of Market Power,* Copyright 1974, Ballinger Publishing Company, p. 23.

Except for a brief period from 1961 to 1962, IBM's share continued to decline until late 1964. It was at this time that the third generation of computers based upon integrated circuits was being developed. Unlike transistors, the advantages of integrated circuits were not great enough to force an immediate change as soon as they were economically feasible. IBM entered the third generation of computers with the System 360 based upon hybrid integrated circuits; this was an intermediate step between discrete component technology and monolithic integrated circuits. The choice of hybrid circuits freed IBM from committing a new product line to an uncertain technology. The System 360 was a success, and IBM's share began rising.[52]

In the mid-1950's, Douglas was the dominant firm in the production of commercial aircraft. At the time the technology for jet aircraft became feasible, all of its capacity was required to meet orders for the piston-engine DC-6's and DC-7's. A prototype jet that Boeing had time to develop enabled them to sign up early orders. Figure 2 reveals the switch in dominance among aircraft firms. Like the changes in the computer industry, the technology for the new generation of aircraft was developed outside the industry.[53]

Figure 2.   Market Share, Major Commercial Aircraft Developers, 1957-1965*

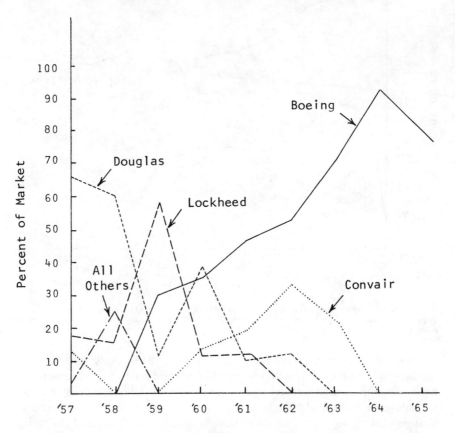

* Source: Almarin Phillips. *Technology and Market Structure.* Lexington, Mass.: D.C. Heath, 1971. Quoted in Burton H. Klein. *Dynamic Economics.* Cambridge: Harvard University Press, 1977, p. 129.

   In both the computer industry and the commercial aircraft industry, firms were able to establish dominance during the transition to a new technology. Even after establishing a dominant position, IBM's market share began declining when it was slow to adopt another technological development. Boeing's dominance is sufficiently recent that it has not had to respond to another major technological change. It did, however, quickly follow introduction of the 707 with the 720 and 727 which solidified its position, and it captured the lead in wide-body jets with the 747.

We hypothesized that dominance would be easy to establish in a high-technology product but difficult to maintain. Both Boeing and IBM found that a change in technology provided an opportunity for dominance. The maintenance of that position required that they constantly respond to new technological advances. Eastman Kodak avoided this by generating changes itself. A "succession of changes and improvements" was the strategy which Kodak followed in establishing and maintaining its position. Its stream of product innovations served to sustain demand and to keep it ahead of competition. In office correspondence with Eastman Photo Materials Co., George Eastman outlined his strategy of a series of quick product changes in order that Kodak might remain the leader in its field. Eastman felt that it was important for the company to introduce improved products, as often as every year, and if the company was able to accomplish this, competitors would be unable to keep up with their pace.[54] In 1890 alone, four new models of the Kodak and three models of the folding Kodak were introduced.

A technological change may help a firm maintain its position as long as the change is being generated internally. External change, however, can jeopardize the market position of an established dominant firm by facilitating entry. To persist, a dominant firm must control the pace of change. Kodak did this, but Douglas did not. Technological change will not necessarily alter the market structure; one dominant firm may simply replace another, as in the case of Boeing and Douglas.

We further hypothesized that firms producing branded consumer products would find market power more difficult to acquire. To the extent that product loyalty is an important factor in their dominance and that it takes time to generate, this will be true. Dominance for these firms will be long-lived if it depreciates slowly. This is likely to be the case if the rate of change in the industries is relatively slow such that the firms do not have to respond frequently to new product competition.

Among the four producers of consumer products in the sample, Gillette, Campbell, and Procter & Gamble were associated with the introduction of a new product. In two instances the production functions were radically changed: the safety razor altered the way the product "shaving" was delivered, and soup was no longer a home production item. The switch from soap to synthetic detergent eventually made possible automatic washing machines, but this was later; initially there was just a switch from one cleaning method to another. Coca-Cola, on the other hand, was one of a number of soft-drink producers making similar products.

Gillette, Campbell, and Procter all held patents associated with the production of their new goods, although in Procter's case it would not have prevented entry.[55] Both Gillette and Campbell held important protected market positions for a number of years as a result of an innovation, and to this extent their dominance was "easy" to establish. Because change was relatively slow after the initial development of the product, they were able to maintain their position by focusing on marketing and product loyalty. There were two aspects to the generation of product loyalty; first, to establish a brand position for protection from imitation after patent expiration and, second, to develop a preference for the new method of delivering the good "shaves" or "soup." Gillette was careful in its early advertising campaigns not to antagonize barbers by emphasizing that the safety razor allowed you to be well-groomed every day.[56] Campbell had to compete with home cooking. The criteria by which consumers judge a convenience food include its quality relative to home cooking, the time saving, the price relative to home cooking, and the convenience in packaging and preparation. In its advertising, Campbell emphasized quality and the special formulation of its products. It took pains to establish strong brand loyalty through devices such as using a unique red ink on all Campbell products and advertisements.[57]

Both Gillette and Campbell may be thought of as initiators of product change in establishing their dominance. Procter & Gamble also brought about change but its situation is different in that it already held a strong position in a related product, soap. By leading the switch, it was able to increase its market share as revealed in table 15. Procter had the added advantage of having an established sales force for marketing. Detergents were simply an addition to its product line. The strategy of Procter which ensured its dominance is more accurately described as product proliferation rather than product loyalty. Procter did not market products under one brand name, but rather each product was promoted as a separate brand. This avoided externalities that one "bad" product might generate. It also meant that Procter products "competed" with each other. Table 16 presents market share data in the heavy-duty detergent market by brand and producer. Notice that Tide's share declined as a result of the introduction of other Procter products, such as Cheer and Dash, but that the total share of Procter increased from 49.0% in 1948 to 58.0% in 1956.

The acquisition of dominance by firms producing branded consumer products was in general the result of invention/innovation, patents/secrecy, and product loyalty. The firms had to create an industry demand in addition to a preference for their particular product because of their innovations. Patents gave the firms time to develop loyalty without having to respond to competition. Once established, dominance proved durable. The fact that industry demand and product demand were created simultaneously strengthened the association between the two and augmented product loyalty. Procter & Gamble is an exception in one sense: it has not relied on the "Procter" brand name but has introduced a steady flow of products instead. Procter pushes each product individually, the result being that if one product fails, there is always another one available.

Table 15.   Market Shares in Soap and Detergents, 1925-1951*

		Soap		
Firm	**1925**	**1937**	**1947**	**1951**
Procter & Gamble	30	40	37	40
Lever	9	22	19	21
Colgate	27	18	19	14

	Synthetic Detergents		
Firm	**1949**	**1950**	**1951**
Procter & Gamble	66	67	69
Lever	6	11	10
Colgate	20	15	14

* Source: Redbook Magazine. *Household Soaps and Synthetic Detergents: Notes on the Industry and Market.* New York: Redbook Magazine Market Research Department, 1958.

Conclusion

Schumpeter argued that the most important form of competition came from the new product and the new organization, and these case studies support his thesis. The common thread which runs through the histories of all of these firms is change and how they generated and responded to it. All of the firms played an active role in the acquisition of their dominance. In no case did dominance appear pre-determined; its acquisition required the interaction of a number of factors. Preliminary evidence indicated that the ease of creating market power varied by product type as a result of the frequency of change in the industries.

The corollary to Schumpeter's argument is that new forms of competition, new products, and new organizations can also jeopardize market power. Some of the firms in this sample have been able to maintain their dominance and others have not. In the following chapters we shall examine the behavioral patterns of the firms to see how they have responded to competition and how their behavior has affected their market power.

Table 16. Estimated Share of Heavy-Duty Packaged, Liquid Detergent Market, 1948-1960

	1948	1949	1950	1951	1952	1953	1954	1955	1956	1957	1958	1959	1960
Total Procter & Gamble	49.0%	53.0%	57.0%	57.2%	57.0%	57.1%	55.5%	55.6%	58.0%	59.0%	58.2%	56.0%	56.7%
Oxydol	17.6	15.2	11.7	9.5	0.9	0.6	N.A.						
Tide	13.1	23.3	33.1	35.1	35.0	30.7	31.5	31.8	30.4	30.8	30.3	29.1	28.3
Duz Soap	14.3	14.5	11.7	10.1	7.7	6.6	5.3	4.2	3.6	2.9	2.0	1.4	1.2
Cheer	--	N.M.	0.5	2.5	7.1	13.5	13.3	12.9	11.9	12.1	12.2	12.3	11.7
Oxydol Synthetic	N.M.				1.3	5.7	5.3	4.6	5.1	5.3	5.7	5.2	5.3
Pink Dreft	N.M.							3.0	3.1	2.7	2.1	1.7	1.5
Duz Synthetic	N.M.								1.0*	1.6	1.4	1.0	2.0
Dash	N.M.						0.1	0.5	2.6	3.2	3.8	4.9	6.3
American Family Detergent	N.A.								0.3	0.4	0.7	0.4	0.4
American Family Flakes	N.A.												
Salvo	N.M.												
Total Lever (excluding total "All")	22.3%	22.4%	23.3%	21.6%	19.4%	17.8%	17.7%	16.1%	16.1%	16.3%	16.5%	15.9%	14.0%
Rinso Blue	N.M.					N.M.	2.0	4.1	4.3	3.8	3.5	3.4	3.1
Surf	1.1	3.0	6.3	7.6	6.3	5.4	5.3	3.7	2.9	2.3	1.9	1.8	1.8
Breeze Synthetic	N.M.				2.4	4.4	4.6	4.2	3.7	4.0	4.1	3.8	3.2
Silver Dust Blue	N.M.						N.M.	0.7	2.1	2.4	2.3	2.4	1.9
Silver Dust Soap	3.5	5.2	5.4	5.0	4.0	3.5	2.7	1.5	0.1	N.A.	N.A.	N.A.	N.A.
Rinso Soap	17.7	14.2	11.6	9.0	6.7	4.5	3.1	1.9	1.3	0.8	0.5	0.4	0.2
Wisk	N.M.												
Vim	N.M.												
"All" (Condensed and Fluffy combined)	N.M.									3.3	5.8	6.5	6.9
Liquid "All"	N.M.												
Total Colgate	13.7%	11.5%	7.8%	8.6%	11.6%	11.2%	11.7%	12.0%	11.2%	9.8%	10.2%	11.5%	11.0%
Fab	3.2	5.1	3.7	5.5	9.4	10.1	10.8	10.4	9.1	7.7	7.9	8.1	8.3
Super Suds Soap	10.5	6.4	4.1	3.1	2.2	1.0	0.3	N.I.	N.I.	N.I.	N.A.	N.A.	N.A.
Ad								1.1	1.7	1.5	1.7	2.6	2.0
Super Suds Synthetic	N.M					0.1	0.6	0.5	0.4	0.6	0.6	0.8	0.7
Octagon	N.A.												
Kirkman's	N.A.												
Monsanto													
"All" Total	N.A.					3.5	4.8	5.8	5.3	2.2	N.M.	N.M.	N.M.
All Others	15.0%	13.1%	11.9%	12.6%	12.0%	10.4%	10.3%	10.5%	9.4%	9.4%	9.3%	10.1%	11.4%

Source: A.C. Nielsen Co. food store data, adjusted to all outlets by Lever projection factors, cited by Lawrence Bernard, "Couldn't Compete Without All, Says Lever President." Reprinted with permission from the January 21, 1963 issue of *Advertising Age.* Copyright 1963 by Crain Communications, Inc., p. 78.

*Estimated by Lever Brothers
N.M. Not Marketed
N.I. Less than 0.1% but measurable
N.A. Not available

4

Price Behavior

Once a firm acquires a dominant position, it faces constantly changing supply and demand conditions and strategic moves by other firms to which it must respond. For some firms market power proves to be a temporary condition while others maintain it for seventy or eighty years. In this and the following chapter, we shall examine the conduct of a sample of dominant firms to gain insights into the persistence of market power for some firms but not others. The discussion in the previous chapter indicated that the acquisition of dominance itself required the active participation of the firms; its maintenance is unlikely to follow unless the firms continue to "invest" in market power through various competitive strategies.

Conduct affects the evolving market structure in two ways. It can directly affect the number of sellers through barriers to entry, predation, or changes in the cost structure. It can indirectly affect market structure by altering the supply and demand conditions which generate that structure. For example, firm behavior determines the underlying product technology, rate of growth of demand, and prevailing marketing methods.

The term "conduct" encompasses a variety of possible competitive strategies: pricing behavior, investment in capacity, research and development policies, and new product introductions. In this chapter we shall examine firm price behavior, and in the following chapter we shall examine non-price policies. In both cases, the main issue will be how these policies generate market structure.

The earliest discussions of dominant firms are found in the context of price leadership models, and later treatment of them has continued to focus on their price policies. More recent research has applied limit pricing analysis. Modeling a dominant firm facing expansion by the fringe and modeling a monopolist facing a potential entrant are similar. In the following two sections we shall examine whether the behavior predicted by these models is observed in the sample. The last part of this chapter will contain an analysis of the structural effects of these strategies.

Price Leadership

In the standard price leadership model, the dominant firm controls industry price and its own output. It determines its demand curve by subtracting the fringe output from industry demand and sets the price which maximizes its profit subject to that demand curve. The fringe "follows" this price and produces the level of output which maximizes their own profit at that price.

Price leadership is not an accurate description of dominant firm behavior. In the aircraft industry and the soft drink industry there are forms of price leadership but not of the kind suggested in the standard model. The relationship between the sellers and buyers in both industries prevents it. Coca-Cola controls only the price of syrup to bottlers and thus indirectly sets price. Boeing's customers hold market power on the buyer side and prevent it from setting price as in the standard model.

In the market for commercial aircraft there are only a few buyers. Past negotiations over initial orders of each new generation of planes were extensive, and the airlines were able to exact substantial concessions from the aircraft makers. These concessions were not always in terms of price; Boeing redesigned the 707 for American Airlines so that it was one inch wider than Douglas's DC-8, and General Dynamics accepted a "$25 billion" down payment from American with twenty-five DC-7's worth only one-half that amount. This form of price behavior is a function of the cost structure in the industry as well as the number of buyers and sellers. Economies of scale and learning effects can be realized by the firm receiving large orders. There is incentive to give price concessions to acquire large initial orders. During the introduction of jet aircraft it was not until the large airlines had placed their first orders that there was any upward price leadership.[1] Convair raised prices first. About a year later both Boeing and Douglas increased prices at the same time—Boeing by 4% to 6% and Douglas by 5%. Convair did not follow them; its 880 continued to sell for $3.6 to $3.8 million. The DC-8 and 707 both sold for $5 to $6 million.[2]

The product of the Coca-Cola company, flavoring syrup, is an intermediate good in the production of the final good, "soft drinks." Coca-Cola has control only over the pricing of the syrup. The case price of Coke is a local decision made by bottlers on the basis of their costs and competition; it varies as much as 70% from one region to another.[3] The current contract between Coca-Cola and its bottlers fixes the price of syrup itself and adds a differential based on sugar price fluctuations. Coke would like to negotiate a new contract which would allow it to raise the price of syrup as the Consumer Price Index changes. The main reason behind this change is that it feels it needs more money for advertising in order to compete with Pepsi. Pepsi itself would like to see the change.

We stand to gain (from the new Coke contract) by having a better competitive freedom to move up in price than we'd have if Coke continued to have their ceiling," said Gerald J. Fisher, PepsiCo's vice president, corporate development. "Whenever the leader is held down that can be disadvantageous to the whole industry."[4]

Coke thus serves as a price leader of a sort. Because Coke is constrained by the bottler contract, Pepsi has less pricing freedom in the upward direction. There is no evidence that Coca-Cola's pricing decisions would prevail if both firms were free to move.

While the fringe firms may not follow the price set by the dominant firm in the manner suggested by price leadership models, they may use the dominant firm's price as a guide and price down from it. This pattern is possible when the dominant firm has been able to differentiate its product. Both Campbell Soup and Procter & Gamble command a price premium over rival brands as does Eastman Kodak.

Other films may sell as much as 30% below Kodak. The standard price leadership model suggests that the dominant firm maximizes profit subject to a demand and marginal revenue curve from which the fringe supply curve has been subtracted. Kodak officials deny taking competitors' products into account in their pricing decision:

Q. In connection with Kodak product pricing during this period of time [December 1958-January 1963, when the witness was a Vice Presdent of the company, sharing responsibility for direction of U.S. sales and advertising, Tr. 2022] was consideration given to the pricing of competitive products?
A. No. I don't really know what you're getting at. We didn't price, you know with consideration of other products that were on the market. We priced from what we thought we could do the best and give us the greatest customer acceptance.
Q. As far as you know has that continued to be the general pricing policy of Kodak?
A. Yes. I believe so.[50]

Kodak's gross profit margins on the Instamatic line of film run as high as 40%. In terms of a mark-up for this film, the company suggests a $1.40 retail price when the manufacturing costs are estimated to be in the neighborhood of 25 cents.[6]

Pricing down from the dominant firm's product is also the pattern price competition takes in the data processing industry. On January 31, 1979, IBM announced less expensive but more powerful CPU's known as the 4300 Series for use in the System 370 product line. NCR and Burroughs waited for IBM to commit itself to a price before following with their own announcement a month later. Both NCR and Burroughs positioned themselves above IBM's less powerful model and below IBM's most powerful model. Thus for comparable products they price down from IBM, and for products they think are better they price above it.[7]

Table 17. A Comparison of Similar Product Line Additions by Three
Computer Manufacturers*

Firm Model	Number of Characters of Main Storage	Price	Price per Megabyte of Additional Memory
IBM			
4331 Model 11	500,000	$ 65,000	$15,000
4341 Model K1	2 million	$245,000	$15,000
NCR			
V-8555M	500,000	$ 88,035	$20,000
		($2,363/mo., 3-yr. lease)	
V-8585M	1 million	$225,300	$20,000
		($5,848/mo., 3-yr. lease)	
Burroughs			
B-2930	524,000-1 million	$140,000	$14,000
B-3950	2 million-5 million	$230,000	$14,000

* Sources: Peter J. Schuyten. "NCR Unveils Computers to Compete with IBM." *New York Times,* 2 March 1979, pp. D1, D4;
Jerry A. Tannenbaum, "IBM Introduces New Processors for System 370," *Wall Street Journal,* Eastern edition, 31 January 1979,
p. 2; "Burroughs Unveils 2 Computer Models in Reaction to IBM," *Wall Street Journal,* Eastern edition, 23 February 1979, p. 25.

In the market for peripherals, IBM products also command a premium
over that of the fringe producers. Between 1968 and 1972 Telex products were
listed at lower prices than IBM products except on four occasions. Telex and
the other plug compatible manufacturers' prices were actually lower than their
list prices due to various price concessions. Even when IBM announced price
reductions on products such as the 2314 and 2319 disk drives, Telex lowered its
prices to maintain a position below that of IBM. An example of Telex price
concessions arose in evidence presented in the *Telex vs. IBM* trial.

> Mr. Pfeiffer, President of IBM's Data Processing Division, reported: "Telex is actively
> marketing their new 1403 plug compatible printer. It is faster, cheaper and has unique on-line
> or off-line capability. On top of these advantages, Telex offers unlimited use versus our 30%
> additional use charge on the 1403. This raises the Telex discount from 25% to 40%...."[8]

While fringe firms do not necessarily take the price of the dominant firm as
given and price accordingly, nevertheless, they are influenced by it. It partially
determines what they are able to charge for their own products. The dominant
firm, on its part, generally discounts the fringe in its decisions.

Limit Pricing

In the previous section we examined the ability of dominant firms to function
as price makers and the adjustment of other firms to their price. The corollary
issue is the level at which they set price. One possibility is that they limit price.

Limit pricing is a theory of how firms strategically use their power to set price to alter market structure. It was originally used to explain the behavior of a monopolist facing potential entry. Given market demand and long-run cost conditions, the monopolist sets price such that after entry the new firms earn no excess profits. This same scenario can be used to describe the behavior of a dominant firm facing expansion by the fringe. It implies that the dominant firm does not set price to maximize current profit but rather some undefined notion of long-run profits.

There is some evidence that IBM attempted limit pricing in memory devices. On August 2, 1972, as part of its "SMASH" program, IBM cut memory price from $12,000 per month per megabyte to $5,200 per month per megabyte—a 57 percent reduction. This action was the culmination of several studies concerning protection of IBM's installed base of memory devices from replacement by plug compatible memory units. IBM's analysis showed that if a new company began hiring in June 1970 and did not ship its first memory until July 1972, it would not break even until 1974 if IBM priced at $16-$18,000 per month per megabyte. At $12,000 it would not break even until 1976. For an established component company, break-even would occur in 1973 with the $18,000 price and in 1975 with a price of $10,000-$12,000. IBM adopted the price of $12,000 for System 370/155 and 165 memory. By March 1971, IBM became concerned that these forecasts had been in error. Another task force to study the issue was created. The final decision was to raise CPU prices and cut memory prices, as reflected in the 1972 "SMASH" announcement. At the *Telex vs. IBM* trial, B.H. Hochfield, an IBM analyst, testified that he felt this price would prevent competition from entering and thus constituted limit pricing. However, other evidence was introduced which showed that peripheral companies would be viable selling at a price as low as $3,000 per megabyte per month.[9]

Darius Gaskins has developed a dynamic version of the limit price theory. In it the dominant firm recognizes the dependence of future market share on current price level and chooses an optimal price trajectory that may allow induced entry rather than simply preserving the current market share. Gaskins also allows for various cost and demand assumptions, that is, he estimates the price trajectories assuming high or low cost advantages of the dominant firm vis-à-vis the fringe and also assuming demand is growing.

In Gaskins's dynamic limit pricing model, there are certain cost and demand conditions under which the optimal price strategy is not the limit price in the usual sense of the term. For example, a producer with little cost advantage would sacrifice market share by adopting a price that declines through time. If a producer's cost advantage erodes over time through a decline in product differentiation, the optimal price pattern also declines continuously toward long-run average total cost.[10]

Eastman Kodak has exhibited a form of dynamic limit pricing. It entered the market for microfilm hardware at a price high enough to attract entrants. When the market became overcrowded, Kodak offered expanded service which had two consequences: it changed the nature of the product offered, and it was an effective price reduction.[11] Whether Kodak's cost advantage was due to production cost differences or product differentiation, its strategy was as Gaskins predicted: a high initial price followed by a lower effective price with a concomitant decrease in market share. Notice that Kodak's strategy was effective because it had the ability to alter the "product" as well as the price. The use of product changes as a competitive device will be examined in chapter 5 in more detail.

Gaskins also examined the effect that variation in a firm's cost conditions relative to its competitors would have on its pricing strategy. A good example of this situation is when a firm faces the expiration of a strong patent position. The optimal price trajectory after expiration depends upon the degree of market penetration by competitors during the protected period. If the firm has a moderate cost advantage as a result of the patent, its optimal path, $p^*(t)$, is as depicted in figure 3. $\overline{P}$ is the limit price at which net entry is zero prior to patent expiration, and c is average total cost and therefore the limit price when the patent is no longer active. The optimal price declines through most of the patent life but reaches a peak at time T. Following expiration it continues to decline toward c.[12] Patents were important factors in the acquisition of dominance in this sample of firms, so this is a possible pricing pattern for them. Gillette displayed similar behavior. It prepared for patent expiration by developing a low-priced razor in order to tap a wider market. This is a variant of the behavior predicted by Gaskins—Gillette did not simply lower the price, it developed a low-priced product. Gaskins's model also predicts a declining market share following patent expiration, but Gillette was able to maintain its position by using the largest advertising campaign in the company's history and carefully managed dealer relationships to protect itself from "imitators."[13] It essentially invested in another base of market power—product loyalty. The model does not fit the behavior of any other firms in the sample. Because their dominance was a result of the interaction of a number of factors, patent expiration did not force the price behavior predicted.

Traditional limit pricing theory does not accurately characterize the pricing behavior of this sample of firms. Gaskins's dynamic version did somewhat better; both Kodak and Gillette displayed variants of the behavior it predicted. The difficulty with applying his model is that real firms are not limited to price as a competitive device. Kodak and Gillette effected price reductions by altering their products. In Kodak's case this meant expanded service, and in Gillette's case a low-priced version of the product was developed. In the next chapter we shall examine non-price behavior in more detail.

Figure 3.   Pricing Strategy for a Firm Holding a Patent*

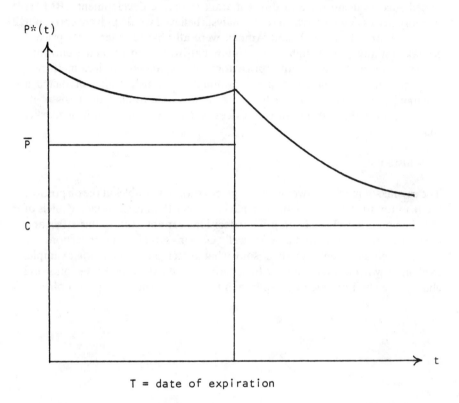

T = date of expiration

* Source: Darius W. Gaskins, Jr. "Dynamic Limit Pricing by Dominant Firms." Ph.D. dissertation, University of Michigan, 1970.

Structural Effects of Pricing Strategies

The reason for examining firm behavioral patterns such as pricing is to determine how that behavior affects the evolving market structure—in particular, how the behavior of firms affects the persistence of a dominant firm structure. Price leadership theory suggests no direct connection between the predicted behavior and market structure. The fringe firms are assumed to face rising marginal costs that keep them from expanding. Limit pricing, on the other hand, is as much a theory about market structure as it is a theory about pricing. The dominant firm employs price to preserve the market structure in the early versions of the theory, or as in Gaskins's dynamic model, it maximizes the present discounted value of its profit stream even if this implies induced entry.

From the evidence on price policies above, dominant firms have had mixed success using price to direct market structure development. IBM set memory prices at a level which some analysts believed would prevent entry, but Telex, Control Data, Itel, and Ampex were all able to enter at its price.[14] Kodak initially priced high in microfilm hardware and attracted entrants. When it lowered the effective price through expanded service, inefficient producers left the market. Finally, although Gaskins's model predicted a declining market share in Gillette's case, it was able to alter the basis of its market power through non-price devices and to prevent erosion of market share.

Conclusion

The essence of market power is that it places several variables at the disposal of the firm for strategic competitive behavior rather than price alone. Models of firm behavior based solely on pricing decisions cannot capture this effect and consequently do not predict very well. Gaskins's model, by incorporating factors such as patents, predicts somewhat better but cannot, for example, explain how firms alter products to achieve a price reduction. In the following chapter we shall broaden our approach to include firms' non-price policies.

5

Non-Price Behavior

As indicated at the outset, the dominant firm is one that through its own individual actions is able to control, to a significant degree, the competitive environment in which it and all other firms in its market operate. One tool for control is price, but other aspects of firm behavior, such as research and development policies, product policies, and vertical integration, also alter the environment. This chapter continues the investigation of the conduct of a sample of dominant firms begun in chapter 4. It will focus on non-price behavior as a means of influencing market structure development and hence the persistence of dominance.

The dominant firm's non-price behavior affects the competitive environment in several ways. The cost structure of the industry or the level of entry barriers is altered by its policies toward vertical integration, research and development, or diversification. Product policies, innovation strategies, and marketing methods change the nature of the "product" itself and therefore the definition of the market.

It is important to recognize that non-price strategies are not available to non-dominant firms. In addition to having the means to control the competitive environment, the dominant firm also determines the nature of the market association itself. Its product defines the market and sets standards that other firms must meet. It can redefine the market when it changes its product, but non-dominant firms would only be removing themselves from "the market" if they attempted a similar strategy. To the extent that marketing strategies also define the product in the eyes of the consumer, they will have a different effect when employed by dominant rather than non-dominant firms.

Non-price policies generally have greater long-run implications for the competitive environment than price policies because they are not as easily reversible. As such, their possible feedbacks from conduct to structure are more important. A discussion of the structural implications of non-price behavior will be delayed until chapter 6.

This chapter will be organized in the following manner. In the first five sections, non-price behavior of dominant firms will be examined in detail and possible behavioral differences due to product type will be identified. The last section will contain a summary and conclusions.

Product Strategies

Product strategies can take many different forms, but the behavior exhibited by this sample of dominant firms falls into four broad categories: policies related to product "proliferation," product change, product alteration as a substitute for price change, and product quality. All four have both long- and short-run consequences for the competitive environment of an industry. In the short-run, competitors must respond to them and make similar strategic moves, while in the long-run they set the tone of industry competition.

Because other firms compete primarily with the dominant firm's product and its product defines the market, it determines the product characteristics upon which competition is based. For example, it can establish multiple varieties of a product or a succession of product changes as the prevailing mode of competition. Other firms in the market may also introduce varieties of products or make a series of changes in their product without the dominant firm making a similar move, but they will not necessarily be profit-maximizing or satisfying strategies for them. If a non-dominant firm adopts a strategy of product proliferation the action may raise its production and marketing costs without it reaping the potential benefits a dominant firm might receive in the form of an expansion of demand or the creation of barriers to entry. The feedbacks from conduct to the competitive environment will be examined in detail in chapter 6. Here we shall simply review the ways in which product strategies manifest themselves in the behavior of this sample of firms.

Product "Proliferation"

Product "proliferation" refers to firm policies which increase the number of products of a similar nature marketed by one firm. It can manifest itself through increases in the number of brands a company offers, the number of models of a given product, or the number of varieties or flavors of a general kind of product. The policy of any one dominant firm may not fall strictly into one of these categories. For example, a firm may produce a number of "flavors" of its product. If they are marketed under one brand name it would constitute "variety" rather than brand proliferation.

The distinction between variety and model proliferation is best understood by an example. Campbell markets many types of soup under one brand name which is a form of variety proliferation. Eastman Kodak, on the other hand, produces a line of similar cameras with different options and prices, a form of model proliferation. While some may simply consider chicken and barley soup a "model" which contains different amounts of various ingredients from chicken and rice soup, we have distinguished this form of "variety" proliferation from "model" proliferation for two reasons. First, varieties generally are marketed differently from models. That is, they are marketed individually while models are marketed as a group. Second, the development expenses related to the two types of proliferation strategies may differ; it may cost relatively less to add or subtract options from a product than to create new varieties of a product.

Model, variety, and brand proliferation are a useful classificatory scheme because their possible competitive effects differ. The introduction of many different models may be a means for a firm to differentiate its product while brand proliferation may create barriers to entry. This is not to imply, however, that a given act of proliferation has only one consequence. The same act of model proliferation or brand proliferation can also expand demand. These effects will be discussed in detail in the chapter concerning the feedbacks from conduct to structure.

Procter & Gamble and Coca-Cola are two dominant firms in the sample that have employed brand proliferation. Both introduce different brands of the same type of product, be it detergents or soft drinks, that have minor differences in their attributes. In both instances, competitors have adopted similar strategies.

Procter's addition of Cheer to its product line was the beginning of its brand proliferation in detergents. The strategy was designed both to increase the shelf space held by Procter regardless of brand, and to appeal to people who did not like Tide; the result was an expansion of the demand for Procter products in particular and detergents in general. This is now a common practice among all of the detergent producers.

> ...[M]anufacturers commonly offer more than one brand at the same time because it is thought that no one brand of detergent will satisfy every housewife and that the best way to increase a company's share of a particular market may be to launch a second or third brand. This policy also provides a reserve brand should the better established one start to slip, as well as giving a company more space on a supermarket's shelves than would otherwise be obtained.[1]

In general, Procter introduces new brands rather than incorporating additional features such as hi- and low-sudsers and water softeners into current products.[2] It also uses the introduction of new brands to direct attention away from existing products that are facing tough competition. Procter's introduction of Top Job is a case in point. The market for all-purpose cleaners contained Lestoil, Handy Andy, and Mr. Clean, a Procter product, when Colgate launched Ajax All-Purpose Cleaner. Procter & Gamble retaliated by introducing Top Job, an ammoniated cleaner like Ajax. Rather than adding ammonia to Mr. Clean, Procter added a new product to its line that embodied this feature. The second Procter entry cut into Handy Andy, Lestoil, and Ajax sales through the advantage of its new label. Top Job became the leading product in the market, but it did not perform as well relative to the other products as Mr. Clean did before the introduction of Ajax.[3]

Firms in the soft-drink industry have the opportunity of employing a form of brand proliferation through the introduction of new flavors, but Coca-Cola has only recently begun exploiting this potential.[4] It was late entering the diet drink market which Royal Crown Cola pioneered.[5] More importantly, it originally was slow to introduce another product in a category in which it already had one entry, even if the second product embodied new features. When Coca-Cola acquired Minute Maid, part of its on-going research involved finding a flavor essence to kill cyclamate after-taste. Fresca was the result, but Coke did not market Fresca since it already had TAB in the diet category.[6] Table 18 details Coca-Cola's recent flavor introductions. In addition to adding new brands such as Mr. PiBB and Mellow Yellow, it is also introducing new flavors in old product lines, such as TAB.

Table 18.   New Flavor Introductions by Coca-Cola*

Year	Product
1960	Fanta line (8 flavors)
1961	Sprite
1963	TAB (low calorie)
1966	Fresca (low calorie)
1973	Mr. PiBB (regular and sugar-free)
1974	Sprite (sugar-free)
	TAB (sugar-free, 8 additional flavors)
1979	Mellow Yellow
	Hi-C soft drinks

*   Sources: Company annual reports; Securities and Exchange Commission, *Form 10-K, The Coca-Cola Company for the Fiscal Year Ended December 31, 1976.*

Variety proliferation is the practice of introducing a number of types of a product under one brand name. Coca-Cola employed this strategy with the introduction of a number of flavors in the TAB line. Campbell's has followed a policy of marketing many types of soup under one brand. As an example, during 1977 and 1978 Campbell introduced two condensed soup varieties, eight soup-for-one varieties, four chunky-soup varieties, and two new serving sizes of chunky soup.[7] Campbell has had remarkable success with its product introductions. Within the food industry fewer than 20% of new products survive a two-year shelf test. However, 90% of the foods Campbell introduced in the period from 1960 to 1965 were still in distribution by 1966.[8]

Introducing new models is another form of product proliferation. Kodak, Gillette, and Coca-Cola have all engaged in forms of it.

The product strategy of Eastman Kodak, as it has evolved, is to introduce as few major new models as possible while having a flow of frequent minor changes. In 1963 Kodak introduced the cartridge loading Instamatic. Assorted models and prices appeared, followed by the Pocket Instamatic in 1972. Seven models of that generation were introduced. This strategy is partially a consequence of the nature of demand in the amateur photography market: novelty is crucial, and as cameras age, amateurs buy less film. A flow of small technical improvements serves to stimulate demand.[9]

Gillette offers a wide range of shaving devices as well as various models of each. When a new razor blade or shaving system is introduced, it is soon followed by a premium version of the product that offers an even "closer" shave. The Super Blue Blade followed the Blue Blade in 1960. It had a silicon coating to reduce the adhesion of molecules in the cutting process, yielding a smoother shave.[10] Gillette followed the introduction of its stainless steel double-edged blade in 1963 with a premium "super stainless steel" version in 1965 that embodied an improved alloy. Besides introducing premium versions of existing blades, Gillette has also introduced different types of shavers. The Techmatic (1965) involved a continuous shaving band in a snap-in cartridge, and the Trac II (1975) was a double-bladed shaving cartridge. The Atra (1977) went a step further; it was a pivoting twin-blade razor.[11]

The manner of packaging and method of delivery define various "models" of soft drinks and are important variables in the strategy of Coca-Cola. Soft drinks may be marketed through fountains, vending machines, or retail stores for take-home. Home use drinks, in turn, may be packaged in a number of different ways. Product strategies include the manner of delivery as well as the taste aspects of the product. As we noted above, Coca-Cola has not been aggressive in flavor introductions. It has also been slow to introduce new packaging devices. Until 1954, Coke was available only in 6-1/2 ounce bottles. At that time it introduced 10- and 12-ounce returnable bottles.[12] The first soft drinks in cans were marketed in 1953, and within a year twenty-five firms offered canned drinks. Coca-Cola did not adopt canned drinks until 1960—the last major producer to do so.[13] In terms of the method of delivery, Coke's market strength has always been soda fountains and vending machines.[14] Its lack of aggressiveness in packaging has hurt it in the take-home market which represents an increasing portion of soft drink sales.

As a competitive strategy, all of the firms producing branded consumer products exhibited some form of product proliferation. Eastman Kodak, which produces what has been designated a high technology product, also engaged in this behavior. In Kodak's case, the important factor in determining behavior is the nature of demand and the ultimate purchaser.

Product Change

The distinction between a policy of product "proliferation" and one of product change is not a hard and fast one. "Proliferation" is used here to designate a policy of introducing similar products as different brands or models while "product change" refers to the rate and manner of introduction of totally new products or to improvements in old products marketed under the same name. Policies related to product change are important because the product of the dominant firm becomes identified with the industry itself.

By introducing a new product, a company may direct competition away from a product in which its competitors have an advantage. This is a strategy which has been used by Procter & Gamble. When Lever began marketing All and improved it, All became a much stronger competitor for Procter's low-suds detergent, Dash. Rather than "fighting" Lever in that market, Procter & Gamble's strategy was to shift the battle to ground on which Lever would not have an entrenched position. It began investing more in a low-sudsing tablet called Salvo. The strategy worked. The combined market shares of Procter's Dash and Salvo exceeded that of All plus Vim, Lever's tablet.[15]

Rather than introducing a new product, a firm may simply make improvements in old ones. Procter has been able to overcome the product-life cycle through a series of constant product changes. Left unchanged, a product will tend to increase in market share, hit a peak, and begin declining. According to a study by A.C. Nielson Co., eighty-five percent of brands can expect less than three years of success before market share starts declining. Procter seems to have been able to override the product-life cycle with regular improvements and an increasing barrage of advertising. As of 1974 no Procter product had died in the past ten years. Once established, a Procter product is changed in some major or minor way twice a year.[16] O.B. Butler, Vice Chairman of the Board of Procter & Gamble, attributes its brand success to these changes:

> The enduring success of brands like Ivory, Crisco, and Tide does not rest solely on the fact that the original innovation was so significant and so successful that it would endure forever. Such endurance is also based importantly on the fact that these brands have been improved and improved and improved over the years.[17]

Product changes become a competitive device that is important for the dominant firm if its products establish standards and other firms compete with it on the basis of compatibility. The task force set up under H.E. Cooley in 1970 to examine the success plug compatible peripheral manufacturers were having replacing IBM devices reviewed a number of product changes as competitive devices. They considered tactics such as "mid-life kickers," proprietary diagnostics, and special interfaces between peripherals and the CPU as means of protecting IBM peripherals on the 370. "Mid-life kickers" were small improvements as new technologies developed to fragment the market.

Proprietary diagnostics were programs with the ability to distinguish IBM and plug compatible devices and to work only on the IBM devices. The Cooley report further warned against the wide-spread marketing of devices such as IBM's Basic Channel Adapter which standardized the interface between CPU's and peripheral devices, and made the replacement of IBM devices even simpler.[18]

Not all dominant firms necessarily compete through product changes. A conscious policy of competition through new product introduction implies that research and development expenditures should be directed towards the products facing the most competition. Kaysen found no consistent relationship in the behavior of United Shoe in this respect. Instead, its division of research effort parallels the relative importance of various machines in manufacturing.[19]

Product Competition as an Alternative to Price Competition

Product strategies may directly replace price competition in some instances. Firms may introduce price cut products as "new" products rather than reducing the price of "old" ones. This is a way for dominant firms to price discriminate. In chapter 4 we also observed that dominant firms do not compete on the basis of the price of their products. A firm producing a "quality" product may resist a price cut, even when it feels it is needed, if the cuts do not accord with its image of high quality. It may instead offer a "new," lower priced product. Alternatively, firms may compete through product design and packaging rather than on a price basis. Small non-dominant firms are less likely to compete on the basis of quality or to have the funds to engage in packaging competition and are more likely to focus on price as a competitive strategy.

IBM has adopted the policy of introducing price cut products as new products. This strategy generates extra revenue by capitalizing on the lethargy of customers who continue paying higher rent rather than exchanging equipment and taking advantage of a price cut. Two products with identical performance specifications but different prices include the 2314 disk drive which was reintroduced as the 2319 and the 2420-7 tape drive which was reintroduced as the 3420-7.[20] In 1970, 2314 disk drives were combined and repriced as the 2319A disk drive and Integrated File Adapter. IFA was a modified 2314 control unit put within the CPU cover of the IBM 370/145. The program was only for use on the 370/145 machine to allow full rent to be charged on the 2314 drives installed on 360's. As old 2314 spindles were returned from lease, they were repackaged into the 2319A series.[21]

In an attempt to price discriminate, United Shoe developed a new machine. The Alpha wood heeler of USMC faced competition from German machines in the slipper trade. United developed a new heeler—the Model B—

and set low terms on it relative to the Alpha which had the same manufacturing cost. In an attempt to keep the Model B from replacing the Alpha in the shoe trade in general, United set high minimum use levels which only the slipper trade could meet.[22]

Eastman Kodak also used product introductions instead of price cuts, even though it does not make a product that is leased. When other gelatin paper manufacturers were engaged in a price war, George Eastman steadfastly refused to participate in price cutting. Instead, he introduced new brands of paper at lower prices while maintaining the established price on the quality brand.[23] This is the same type of behavior that Gillette exhibited following its patent expiration.

Procter has used product design as an alternative to price competition. In 1959 it introduced Mr. Clean in a 28-oz. bottle and charged as much for it as a 32-oz. bottle of Lestoil. Mr. Clean had the advantage that it was non-flammable and was more conveniently shaped. The smaller bottle of Mr. Clean was designed to look as big or bigger than Lestoil and soon outsold it two to one.[24]

Product Quality

Non-price strategies alter the dimensions along which the "product" is defined, and one of these dimensions is quality. Firms choose to produce a product of a given quality, and this is one non-price competitive stance. We saw, in the examination of this sample's sources of dominance, that product loyalty played a large role and that this loyalty was the result, as often as not, of quality differences. The quality of the product that the firm continues to produce is a discretionary behavioral trait that can continue to affect market structure by differentiating the products of one firm from another.

One of Kodak's sources of dominance was product loyalty due to the quality of its products, and it has continued to compete on the basis of the quality of its product. As of 1963, Eastman was one of 2% of United States businesses that were using scientific methods of quality control according to the American Society for Quality Control. In addition to inspection and process control, that is, efforts to keep wastes and costs at a minimum, quality control at Kodak involves an evaluation to determine if the product will do the job intended. Kodak's vertical integration, to be discussed below, is another way it assures the quality of its products through the quality of inputs. It uses advertising to sell this quality and reliability.[25]

Product quality became a competitive issue in an anti-trust case against Gillette in the mid-1930s. Otto Roth, Inc., a subsidiary of Gillette's German subsidiary, supplied proprietary blades on the U.S. market. A competitor charged that Gillette wanted to push their branded products so they ordered Roth to let quality decline. Although the charge of monopolization was not sustained, testimony was presented that Gillette ordered stroppers removed from Roth machines. In the aftermath of this case, new management at Gillette adopted production of a high quality product as a competitive strategy, and quality rather than price became its advertising point.[26] This remains Gillette's basic policy today. Its ad campaigns follow the lines of "here's what it is and here's how it works." They tend to provide technical information rather than emphasize glamor. Copy for razor blades stresses the number of shaves per blade or how the blades work to provide a better shave.[27]

Coca-Cola produces food products and therefore must appeal to consumers' taste. One way to do this is to produce an item of consistent quality. Soft drinks are not a complex product so quality control is not difficult. One problem Coca-Cola faces, however, is that it does not produce the final product that is delivered to the consumers. The operations of bottlers ultimately determine the degree of standardization of the product. Part of Pepsi's resurgence in the 1950's depended upon standardization of quality from franchise to franchise.[28]

Campbell Soup seeks to appeal to consumers through the quality of its products. Many ingredients are made to Campbell's specifications to insure quality control and to make its product hard to duplicate. Batches of soup are taste tested by top management every morning at Camden, New Jersey. In 1947 the entire tomato juice crop was destroyed because it did not meet taste standards.[29] Despite Campbell's avowed zeal for quality, there appears to be at least one fly in its soup: a Consumers Union test of Swanson products found insect body parts and rodent hair.[30] At Campbell's, quality is the "image," too. It was accused of deceptive advertising practices by the Federal Trade Commission as a result of a series of commercials in which marbles were used to support the solid ingredients of soup, thus giving them a "chunky" appearance.[31]

Quality is used more frequently as a competitive device by firms producing what we have labelled branded consumer products than by those producing high technology products. Eastman Kodak is the exception. The crucial element in this instance seems to be whether the purchaser is a consumer or producer. Consumers are generally less knowledgeable buyers and are more susceptible to suggestions of quality. Although Kodak produces a high technology product, it sells to consumers who are even more likely to have difficulty judging its product than those of Gillette, Campbell, or Coke.

Summary of Product Strategies

Product strategies are a pervasive method of competition in this sample. Seven out of nine firms employed it in some form as a competitive device—only Boeing and Pullman did not. Boeing is constrained by the cost structure in its industry. Substantial economies of scale and learning effects could not necessarily be achieved under a policy of "model" proliferation. There is some use of "stretching" or a modification of a basic design to accommodate more seats. This enables firms to spread development costs further. Technical progress is more important in determining the rate of product change than firm policies. There is some use of product design as an alternative to price competition, but this is a result of buyer pressure rather than being initiated by the firms in the industry. The structure of buyers in the sleeping car industry also determined Pullman's product strategies. Before dissolution the largest buyer of cars from Pullman-Standard was the Pullman Company; it thus had little incentive to resort to product strategies.

Product strategies are used most widely by producers of branded consumer products. All of them exhibited some form of product proliferation. It seems to be a key to the maintenance of their dominance since Coca-Cola, the firm that declined, has only recently begun employing this strategy. Product loyalty was an important source of dominance and product quality, one "source" of loyalty, was employed in the firms' competitive strategies.

Although product strategies are often used by producers of branded consumer goods, some producers of high technology goods also employ them. The purchasers and nature of demand in the amateur photography market make model proliferation, product change in lieu of price change, and product quality useful competitive devices. IBM and United Shoe substitute new product introductions for price changes and in this manner attempt to price discriminate. In addition, IBM uses product changes as competitive devices.

The competitive effects of product policies vary widely. Some have the potential for creating barriers to entry, and others expand demand. These will be reviewed in detail in chapter 6.

Research and Development: Innovation

The earlier statistical analysis of the behavior of dominant and non-dominant firms revealed differences in their patterns of research and development expenditures. In particular we found that dominant firms do significantly more R&D per unit of sales than non-dominant firms. When the firms were examined by product type, technology intensive dominant firms were observed to do significantly more R&D than other consumer-type dominant firms and other technology-intensive non-dominants. Research and development expenditures are, however, only an input into the generation of innovation. It is this output in terms of new processes and products which is of interest. Although we have already demonstrated that dominance leads to more R&D, a flow of new products may not necessarily follow. In this section we shall review selected innovations in the sample of firms' industries.

The three dominant firms which eventually declined—Pullman, United Shoe, and Coca-Cola—did not have outstanding records in the area of innovation. Pullman experimented some with aluminum trains, but they were not as successful as the stainless steel ones created by Budd Manufacturing Co. Pullman's insistence on standardization, although it allowed economies of scale to be reaped in manufacturing and servicing, may have been another bar to innovation.[32] In the 1940 anti-trust case, Pullman's policy was described as "... obdurate resistance to changes in the type of cars pressed for by railroad customers..."[33]

In terms of research effort, United Shoe has a good record. The major objective in its research has been development of new machines with improvement of existing machines a secondary goal. The results, however, have not been spectacular. Labor requirements of shoe manufacture have decreased but not faster than that of manufacturing as a whole. New models appear infrequently. The median age of all models in 1955 was 28 years. Carl Kaysen concluded:

> In short, progress in shoe machinery has not been made by leaps and bounds; rather it is glacial in its character.... United has not met the burden of bringing forth positive acceptable evidence to support its view of the excellence of its own research as being such as both to explain United's position in the market, and to justify whatever practices may be necessary to insure its continuance at its present level.[34]

The most numerous innovations in the soft drink industry have come in packaging. Coca-Cola pioneered in this area in the 1910's and 1920's. It was the first firm to use a unique bottle design for identification in 1915, and it introduced the six-bottle carton, or "home-pack," in 1922.[35] Other innovations are listed in table 19. In recent years, most of these have come from fringe firms. Even if Coke had the technology for a new product, it did not necessarily market it rapidly.

Table 19.   Selected Innovations in the Soft Drink Industry*

Coca-Cola	Fringe
Patented bottle design used for identification	Royal Crown: diet drinks
Six-bottle carton, or "home-pack"	Pepsi: One-way bottle 12-oz. bottle
Lift-off caps	Cantrell and Cochrane: Canned drinks

* Sources: Kenneth C. Fraundorf. "The Social Costs of Packaging Competition in the Beer and Soft Drink Industries." *Antitrust Bulletin* 20 (Winter 1975): 16; John J. Riley. *A History of the American Soft Drink Industry.* Washington, D.C.: American Bottlers of Carbonated Beverages. 1958, p. 143; Ted Sanchagrin. "Private-label Soft Drinks Don't Faze Coke and Pepsi." *Printers' Ink* 292 (April 8, 1966): 16; Jack B. Weiner. "Why Things Go Better at Coke." *Dun's Review* 88 (October 1966): 71.

In comparison, the old dominant firms which maintained their position have made more substantial contributions in their industries in terms of new products. Selected innovations in razors and blades are detailed in table 20.

Gillette has made several substantial new product introductions; in particular, it developed continuous band shavers and double-blade shaving cartridges. The most important contribution of the fringe has been in increasing the pace of Gillette's product introductions. Wilkinson forced it to move more rapidly on the stainless steel blades. The Gillette introduction of microsmooth honing coincided with the Warner-Lambert introduction of a pivoting razor with a cleaning button. Gillette executives "assert" that its development was neither hurried nor delayed as a result of the Warner product.[36]

Table 20.   Selected Innovations in Razors and Blades*

Gillette		Fringe
Coated Blade	Wilkinson Sword:	Stainless Steel Blade
Improved alloy of stainless steel		Bonded razor cartridge
Continuous band shavers	Warner-Lambert:	Magazine razor
Double-blade shaving cartridge		Various injector razor improvements
Pivoting twin-blade razor		Pivoting razor with push-button cleaning system
Honing process, "microsmooth"	Bic:	Disposable razor

* Sources: Walter Guzzardi, Jr. "Gillette Faces the Stainless Steel Dragon." *Fortune* 68 (July 1963): 242; Richard A. Smith. "Gillette Looks Sharp Again." *Fortune* 45 (June 1952): 159; "How Gillette Has Put on a New Face." *Business Week,* 1 April 1967, pp. 58-60; William M. Carley. "Gillette Co. Struggles as its Rivals Slice at Fat Profit Margin." *Wall Street Journal,* Eastern edition, 2 February 1972, p. 14; John J. O'Connor. "Schick, Gillette War Sharpens." *Advertising Age* 49 (November 6, 1978): 1; John J. O'Connor. "Did Gillette Rush Intro of Good News to Avert the Bad?" *Advertising Age* 47 (February 23, 1976): 3, 139; John J. O'Connor. "Schick Promotions Out to Challenge Gillette's Position on Top With Atra." *Advertising Age* 49 (March 20, 1978): 2.

R&D at Campbell's Soup falls into two main categories: basic research on the ingredients that go into the products, and development of new products themselves. A major part of its time is spent studying tomatoes since they are an ingredient in approximately one-half of its total sales volume. Campbell developed tomato strains that are resistant to weather and fungus and are uniform in growing time and color. To disseminate its crop innovations, it grows tomato plants and sells them at cost to farmers as well as providing advice on planting.[37] This research is carried out in agricultural research facilities which Campbell operates. In the area of product innovation, Campbell developed the "Noo" soups and the ready-to-serve "Chunky" soup line. One area in which Campbell did not lead was the development of dry soups.[38]

Eastman Kodak has a varied record in the area of R&D and innovation. From 1879 to 1890 radical innovations interspersed periods of more continuous change. The radical changes in products and production methods included Eastman's invention of dry plates (1879-80), roll holders and paper film (1884-85), and the Kodak camera with nitrocellulose film (1888-89). The first Kodak marketed in June 1888 was a 22-oz. camera that could be used without a tripod. It sold for $25 and came with film for 100 exposures. The camera was sent back to the factory for reloading at a cost of $10. In October of that year, this camera was followed by another model of Kodak which had even larger pictures. The first folding Kodak was marketed in 1890. After this series of innovations, during the remainder of the decade the Eastman company was responsible for fewer of the major innovations. Instead, entrants seeking the Eastman market provided the technical changes.[39] The Blair Camera Company pioneered the placement of film in front of the focal plane of the camera, and Boston Camera Manufacturing Company marketed a daylight cartridge-loading system for front-roll cameras. In photographic paper, Kodak was a follower rather than an innovator. When its scheme to control the raw paper stock failed, Kodak tried to develop new papers in two weak areas of its product line—platinum paper and developing-out paper. In both cases, its efforts were failures, and it was forced to acquire companies with established products.[40]

The incidents related above demonstrate that Kodak was not the only firm which was innovating at this early stage of the photographic industry. Innovation, however, proved to be its most reliable source of market power when control of inputs and patent policies failed. At the same time that Kodak was experiencing the setbacks mentioned above, the foundation for future company policy on technology was being laid. George Eastman, in withdrawing from the technical role he played early in the company's history, succeeded in institutionalizing the process of innovation. He sought technically-trained college graduates who undertook his duties. The staff Eastman developed provided Kodak with the most modern production facilities in the world.[41]

Kodak's commitment to research is still strong. Table 21 gives the R&D expenditures for a number of companies in the photographic industry between 1970 and 1974. Kodak's R&D expenditures as a percent of sales are higher than those of other firms within its own industry at the 5% level of significance.

The commitment of funds to R&D does not automatically result in an output of new products or processes. In table 22, selected innovations of Kodak and other firms in the photographic industry are reviewed. Kodak has undoubtedly been a major souce of new products in the industry. However, part of Kodak's role is due to the systems aspects of photographic products. Its three major innovations in flash devices were jointly developed: Sylvania and Kodak produced the flashcube and magicube, and General Electric and Kodak produced the flipflash. Kodak's market share makes it the logical firm to be approached for these development projects. If Sylvania or G.E. had developed

Table 21. Photographic Industry: Research and Development Expenditures of Selected Companies, 1970-1974*,**

Company	1970	1971	Percent Change	1972	Percent Change	1973	Percent Change	1974	Percent Change
Eastman Kodak	171	180	5.3	215	19.4	248	15.3	274	10.5
Percent of Sales	6.1	6.0		6.2		6.1		6.0	
Xerox Corporation	98	104	6.1	132	26.9	167	26.5	197	18.0
Percent of Sales	5.7	5.3		5.5		5.6		5.5	
3M Company	82	86	4.9	95	10.5	114	20.0	132	15.8
Percent of Sales	4.9	4.7		4.5		4.5		4.5	
GAF Corporation	13	13	0.0	14	7.7	14	0.0	16	14.3
Percent of Sales	2.2	1.8		1.8		1.7		1.7	
Du Pont Company	n.a.	250	—	255	2.0	276	8.2	344	24.6
Percent of Sales		4.7		5.2		4.6		5.0	
Bell & Howell Company	21	19	-9.6	23	21.0	24	4.3	23	-4.2
Percent of Sales	6.6	5.9		6.3		6.1		5.0	

* In millions of dollars.
** Sources: Corporate annual reports. Cited in U.S. Department of Commerce. *The U.S. Photographic Industry 1963-73: An Economic Review.* Washington, D.C.: U.S. Government Printing Office, 1976, p. 55.

the devices with any other producer, they would have been cutting themselves off from the largest part of the camera market. Because of this, Kodak's dominance or large market share may be said to have led to innovations, but it does not imply any other firm was technologically incapable of developing them.[42]

Table 22.   Selected Innovations in the Photographic Industry*

Eastman Kodak	Fringe
X-ray Film	
X-Omat automatic developing machine	Du Pont: Switch from a cellulose
RP X-Omat which further decreased	acetate to a polyester
developing time and expense	base.
Still Camera Equipment	
Instamatic cartridge-loading camera	Polaroid: Instant camera SX-70
"Pocket" Instamatic	Berkey: Electronic flash
Magicube (with Sylvania)	
Flashcube (with Sylvania)	
Flipflash (with General Electric)	
Motion Picture Equipment	
Brownie movie camera	Bell & Howell: Electric eye
Super 8mm movie system	Revere: 8mm Cine zoom
(cartridge film)	
Available light movie camera	
Film videoplayer	
"Ektasound" movie camera	
(records sound directly in	
the camera)	
Film	
Instamatic cartridge film	Polaroid: Instant film
16mm film for pocket camera	SX-70 film
Ektachrome 160 (available	
light motion picture film)	
Reduction in the number of	
processing steps	

*   Sources: Robert Sheehan. "The Kodak Picture—Sunshine and Shadow." *Fortune* 71 (May 1965): 158; "Can Kodak Come up with an Encore?" *Forbes* 102 (November 1, 1968): 37; "Eastman Kodak: What Makes it Click?" *Forbes* 91 (April 1, 1963): 25; U.S. Department of Commerce. *The U.S. Photographic Industry 1963-73: An Economic Review.* Washington, D.C.: U.S. Government Printing Office, 1976, pp. 32-35; *Berkey Photo, Inc. vs. Eastman Kodak Co.*, 457 F. Supp. 404 (1978).

Among the newly dominant firms, the record on innovation is mixed. Procter has been slow creating new product categories. Except for enzymes, it has been late in every major soap and detergent category since Tide: light-duty detergents, deodorant soaps, liquid cleaners, spray cleaners, low-sudsing detergents and medium-sudsing detergents.[43] A major area of innovation in the detergent industry besides new products themselves has been packaging. Here also Procter has been a follower. Lever pioneered in the packaging of soap chips in boxes and in dripless metal cans for liquid detergents. Purex claims to have first developed a plastic bleach jug with a handle; it was also the first company to market an all-plastic cleanser container. Colgate-Palmolive first marketed squeeze cans and moisture-proof containers.[44] Procter's strategy has been to develop "radical" new products in other areas, for example, therapeutic dentifrices and anti-dandruff shampoos, but to follow in detergents.

Although IBM did not invent the computer, it has subsequently been the source of several innovations. Table 23 contains a summary developed by Gerald Brock of selected innovations in the industry. The main conclusion that can be drawn from it is that no one firm, IBM included, has consistently led in technical innovations. IBM's contributions have come in the areas of disk and tape technology and language development. Although they were important, they do not reflect its relative size in the industry. In areas in which IBM did not lead, it has not always been a quick follower.

IBM's progressiveness does not justify its market share, nevertheless, its market share affects its progressiveness in two ways. First, it affects the rate of product introduction under a lease system. If a new product has a low impact on existing products, it may be profitable to introduce it, but if it will only replace old equipment it may be delayed. An IBM management committee determined that a delay of three to six months in the announcement of the System 370 would yield $30 to $50 million in revenue. Also, in considering delivery of a new operating system, IBM determined that the system would be postponed if "the current generation systems are doing so well in the field that there is no compelling business reason for revealing our intentions."[45] Second, IBM's market share enables it to "force" acceptance of IBM innovations whether or not they are technically superior. The decision on a binary coding scheme for data is a good example. A committee of the American Standards Association began in 1959 to study various coding schemes and eventually devised a new one known as ASCII. IBM voted against accepting the code and proposed its own instead. Despite orders by Lyndon Johnson establishing ASCII as a federal standard, it was not widely used. Although IBM failed to get its own code adopted as the standard, it did succeed in containing use of ASCII. Other manufacturers adopted the IBM scheme, and it became a *de facto* industry standard.[46]

In the past Boeing has used a technology base generated by government research in its development of new commercial aircraft. Each generation of civilian transport except the DC-9 and 727 has relied on technology developed for the military, and in their case the broad technology base was government supported.[47] Boeing did lead in adapting a technology developed elsewhere to produce jet aircraft and wide-body jets, but because the rate of technical progress is so strongly affected by factors beyond the control of the individual firms, it is difficult to judge their relative progressiveness.

In summary, innovation is one important strategy for maintaining dominance. Certainly those firms that lost their market power were not important sources of change in their industry. Those firms that maintained their dominance, although important sources of technical change in their industry, did not exhibit a degree of progressiveness concomitant with their market share. The underlying technology of the industry is the most important variable in determining the relative "progressiveness" of the dominant firm. If the pace of technical change is moderate, dominant firms may or may not be industry leaders. Procter has demonstrated the value of rapid copying, and Gillette utilized it also in stainless steel blades. The more rapidly the technology is changing, the less likely it is that the dominant firm is the major force of change in the industry. This is particularly true if part of the technical developments are being generated outside the industry. In such cases, entry is possible in specialized markets. We observed this pattern of competition in the photographic industry during the 1890's and early 1900's and in the computer industry more recently.

Investment Policies

In Chapter 4 firms' use of price to deter entry was examined. Michael Spence has extended this type of analysis to other behavioral attributes of the firm. He argues that investments in industry capacity, advertising, or systems of exclusive dealerships also serve to limit entry. Although his model is strictly applicable to an oligopolistic industry producing a relatively homogeneous product, it suggests variables that dominant firms may also use as limiting devices.[48]

In the pure capacity case, Spence's model predicts capacity above cost minimizing levels at a given output and capacity running ahead of demand in a dynamic world. We have only casual evidence related to the use of capacity for deterring entry. Douglas, which was dominant in commerical aircraft before the rise of Boeing, did not use capacity as a means of limiting entry. One reason for Boeing's ascendency was that Douglas did not have the facilities to develop a jet; it was too busy filling orders for piston-engine aircraft.[49] IBM is not currently using capacity as an entry deterring device. Customers are experiencing delays in delivery of IBM's minicomputer series, the 4300, although this is partially due to an IBM marketing technique—early announcement of products.[50]

Spence suggested that the concept of investment could be extended to other forms of capacity such as the network of bottlers in the soft drink industry. Coke began developing a bottler network in 1904. Other soft drink companies followed suit, and between mid-1930 and mid-1950 the industry became almost totally local in bottling and distribution.[51] The technology of bottling determined this marketing arrangement; glass bottles were fragile and could not easily be shipped long distances. A network of bottlers represents a

Table 23. Selected Innovations in the Computer Industry*

Innovation	Leading company	Date of first delivery	Developer, if other than leading company	Time before IBM delivered
Components				
Transistors	Univac—small scale			
	Philco—large scale	Oct., 1958	Bell Tel. Labs (1948)	14 months
				IBM was 6th firm to enter
Thin film buffer memory	Univac			
Integrated circuits	Scientific Data Systems— small scale	Apr., 1965	Texas Inst.; Fairchild	
	RCA—large scale	Nov., 1965		
Medium scale integration	Data General	Feb., 1969	Semiconductor, Bell Labs, 1959-60	11 months
Semiconductor buffer memory	IBM			
Semiconductor main memory	Data General—small scale	June, 1971		
	AMS—add-on	June, 1971		
	IBM—large scale systems	Sept., 1971		
Operating Systems and Compilers				
Fortran	IBM	1956		
Commercial Language Compiler	Honeywell-Fact		RCA, Univac-Cobol	
Multitasking	Honeywell	1960		
Virtual memory	Manchester University	1959-61		
Multiprocessing	Burroughs	July, 1962 (Military)		
	Burroughs	March, 1963 (Commercial)		

	Company	Date	IBM lag
Time sharing	MIT		
Direct execution of high level languages	General Electric Burroughs	1972	
Architecture Improvements			
Index registers	Burroughs	Jan., 1954	
Buffered input-output	Univac, IBM	Mar./Apr., 1956	
Microprogramming	Manchester University		
Loadable microprogramming	Standard Computer Corp. IBM	Jan., 1967 Jan., 1968	12 months
Input-Output Equipment			
High density tape drives	Storage Technology Corp. 3200 b.p.i. IBM 6250 b.p.i.	1972	12 months
Removable disk packs	IBM	Oct., 1962	
Moving head disk improvements	IBM		
High speed fixed head disks	Burroughs, Control Data Corp.		IBM had not matched as of 1974

Source: Reprinted with permission from Gerald W. Brock. *The U.S. Computer Industry: A Study of Market Power.* Copyright 1974, Ballinger Publishing Co., table 11-1.

substantial investment in "capacity" for any firm desiring to enter or expand. Dr. Pepper has been able to avoid this investment by "piggybacking" on the Coke and Pepsi networks. Franchises are not legally obligated to bottle only the parent company's product. By convincing Coke and Pepsi bottlers to handle its product, Dr. Pepper avoided an extensive investment in capacity.[52]

The changing technology in bottling is now altering the limiting effect of bottling capacity. Canned drinks are produced on high-speed lines that require large volume. Fewer bottles are returnable. King Cola is seeking to enter and eliminate franchising by distributing through supermarket warehouses and food brokers.[53] This strategy would not be possible if the only packaging were returnable bottles.

Vertical Integration

When we examined mergers as a possible source of dominance, we noted that vertical as well as horizontal mergers can create market power. Vertical integration can also be accomplished through an expansion of production facilities within the firm itself. The latter form of vertical integration is more common among this sample of firms.

Kodak began its backward integration as early as the 1890's. Several factors led George Eastman to consider the possibility of supplying basic raw materials within the company.

> Because the requisite raw materials were primarily chemicals that carried high profit margins, at an early point Eastman directed investment of company profits in this direction as a cost-saving measure. Further considerations included better control of the quality of these vital raw materials through the company's own production, and independence from other firms, which might raise prices, halt production because of labor problems, or leak formula secrets to potential competitors.[54]

Integration accomplished through production at Kodak included manufacture of nitrocellulose (1899); sulfuric acid, nitric acid, and fusel oil (1898); developing and toning solutions (early 1900's); boxes for packaging (1890's); and shutters (early 1900's). Capacity in plate glass production was obtained via acquisition in 1903, and raw paper stock was obtained through exclusive contracts.[55] Chemicals proved to be the most important area of vertical integration at Kodak. In 1920, Tennessee Eastman Co. was formed to supply photographic chemicals to Eastman Kodak. Backward integration was pushed even further when Texas Eastman Company was established in 1950 to supply chemical raw materials, primarily alcohols and aldehydes, to Tennessee Eastman.[56] Kodak has also integrated forward into film processing. The developing and printing service was established in the late 1880's and proved an important aspect of company strategy in reaching the mass market since the early Kodak cameras had to be returned to the factory for installation of new film and developing of old.

Increased profit and quality control are common themes in the integration strategies of dominant firms. Campbell Soup began making its own cans in 1954 as a result of judgments in anti-trust suits against American Can and Continental Can that outlawed cumulative quantity discounts.[57] Campbell could no longer exercise its market power as the largest buyer when they were outlawed; it was therefore in its interest to integrate backward. Conversely, Procter & Gamble has not integrated backward into chemicals. There are approximately forty companies supplying materials to soap and detergent makers, although some specialize in only a small area. Table 24 lists some of these firms. Procter has neither the incentive nor the expertise to pursue backward integration. It does have its own sales force—a form of forward integration—rather than selling through food brokers. Coca-Cola has begun to engage in forward integration for the increased profit which it brings. It has acquired bottlers handling approximately ten percent of its volume.[58]

Table 24. Suppliers of Raw Materials in Detergent Manufacture*

Firms Specializing in Detergent Materials
Cowles Chemical
DeSoto Chemical Coatings
Detrex Chemical Industries
Economics Laboratory
Calgon
West Chemical Products
Textize Chemicals

Firms Earning Sizeable Revenue From Detergent Materials
GAF
W.R. Grace & Co.
Pensalt Chemical
Stepan Chemical
Witco Chemical
Wyandott Chemicals
Diamond Alkali

* Source: Joan Green. "Experts in Grime." *Barron's* 47 (April 24, 1967). Reprinted by permission of *Barron's* © Dow Jones & Company, Inc. (1967). All rights reserved.

In an industry with a rapidly changing technology there are compelling reasons both for and against vertical integration. It may reduce "bottlenecks" in the process of technical change by placing more stages under the control of the firm. On the other hand, if technology in one aspect of the production of the good is changing rapidly, the integrated firm may have difficulty keeping up with firms that specialize. In the cases of vertical integration discussed above, the technologies of the areas of integration were relatively established. Among the firms with a more rapidly changing technology, Boeing has chosen not to integrate vertically. Only one firm in the United States has produced both airframes and engines, and it is no longer in business. Instead, engines are produced by firms specializing in them. The industry itself has experienced a rapid rate of change, and a good engine is used by a number of aircraft manufacturers.[59] Another factor that works against integration in commercial aircraft is the relative shortness of production runs. Economies of scale exist in engine production. If aircraft producers developed their own engines, they would not have as many units of output over which to spread development costs as specialized engine firms.

The computer industry exemplifies both positive and negative aspects of vertical integration. IBM produces both hardware and software. When they are simultaneously determined, software may take advantage of any special characteristics of hardware, and trade secrets remain proprietary.[60] IBM has also chosen to produce its own semi-conductors while other companies purchase them. Despite extensive research in the area, in 1968 and 1969 management review committees at IBM found that it was one year behind in logic and two years behind in field effect transistors.[61] While there were advantages to integration into software, IBM experienced disadvantages in semi-conductors.

Diversification

Not all of the dominant firms' expansion had necessarily been in areas of their dominance. Diversification offers firms the opportunity to spread risk, stabilize earnings, or enter a new and rapidly growing market. On the other hand, for firms considering expansion, it is often easier to enter related markets than wholly new industries due to technical expertise and marketing knowledge that carries over to the related product. Related markets also offer the prospect of exporting dominance, that is, using market power in one product to increase it in another area, perhaps through joint marketing or various tie-ins. We hypothesized that dominant firms with large market power and stable earnings would tend to be less diversified, with any expansion occurring in related markets. In chapter 2 we found that a sample of dominant firms had significantly fewer acquisitions than non-dominant firms. The second part of the hypothesis, that dominant firms will tend to move into related product areas, will be examined below.

United Shoe began to diversify following an antitrust decree that altered its marketing method of leases. It first attempted to diversify through invention. United did R&D on a baseball stitching machine, for example, but could not market it. Next came diversification through acquisition. United's "barefoot" or non-shoe business falls into three related market areas: (a) the market for speciality fasteners, an expansion of its eyelet business to include telephone dialing equipment, pop rivets and industrial power tools; (b) specialty industrial chemicals, such as adhesives used in packaging and heat sealing plastics; and (c) specialized industrial machines, such as a machine which presses, cuts, folds, and cements cartons. A number of United's acquisitions were both unrelated to the basic technology of shoe machinery and outside its usual marketing channels. Companies making products such as minicomputers, plastic molding machines, and kites were purchased and written-off as losses in the late 1960's and early 1970's. In 1976 United itself was acquired by Emhart Industries.[62]

Pullman Incorporated also began to diversify following an anti-trust decree that forced divestiture of its operating division, the Pullman Company. Trailmobile and M.W. Kellogg Company, which produce truck trailers and equipment used in the oil, gas, and chemical industries, respectively, were acquired. Subsequent acquisitions have fallen into three main areas:

(1) transportation equipment;

(2) engineering and construction serving the petrochemicals, electric utilities, and metals industries; and

(3) leasing and financing.[63]

Although some of Pullman's acquisitions have been in the field of transportation equipment, others have not. The decline in demand for passenger cars combined with the high variability in demand for all transportation equipment resulted in a move into other product areas.

Both Pullman and United Shoe faced a change in the marketing methods that supported their market power, and this resulted in moves to diversify. The direction in which they diversified was conditioned by the general level of demand for their industries' products as well as their basic technologies and marketing channels. United's successful acquisitions were in areas within its usual marketing channels and of a loosely related technology base. Pullman has moved into other areas because of the volatility of demand in transportation equipment. In its case, market power did not yield stable earnings.

A reason for diversification, other than to achieve stability of earnings, is to move from slow to faster growth industries. Three other firms in our sample are located in slow or low growth industries: Coca-Cola, Gillette, and Campbell Soup. In all cases the nature of demand has provided a stimulus for diversification. Coca-Cola and Campbell Soup have remained in related product areas although Gillette has diversified more widely. Campbell has acquired other prepared food firms and more recently branched into fast food. Coke has acquired orange juice and wine producers. Gillette has tended to acquire products that are impulse purchase or repeat purchase items and are distributed through grocery and variety stores. It is now in the process of pruning calculators and digital watches, two acquisitions that do not fit that pattern.[64]

Table 25. Major Acquisitions by the Sample of Dominant Firms*

Boeing
1960   Vertol Aircraft Co.

Campbell Soup Co.
1921   Franco-American Products
1948   V-8 Cocktail Vegetable Juice (trade name and
        production facilities)
1955   C.A. Swanson and Sons
1961   Pepperidge Farms
1970   Two fast-food chains
1972   Valley Tomato Products, Inc.
        Lexington Gardens
1973   Chain of pizza restaurants
1974   Godiva Chocolates

Coca-Cola
1960   Minute Maid Corp.
1964   Duncan Foods Co.
1969   Belmont Springs Water Co.
1970   Aqua-Chem, Inc.
1975   Thomas (parent bottler network)
        Sterling Vineyards
        Gonzales & Co.
1978   Presto Products

Eastman Kodak
1901   Rochester Optical & Camera Co.
        M.A. Seed Dry Plate Co.
1931   Camera works of Dr. August Nagel
1948   Distillation Products, Inc. (liquidated 1949)
1950   A.M. Tenney Associates (selling agent for
            Tennessee Eastman products)
1966   F.W. Hasselblad & Co.
        C. Hellmund W. & Cia Sucs
1969   J.L. Nerlien A/S (distribution and processing)
1973   Spin Physics (magnetic heads for recording equipment)

Gillette
1930   Autostrop Safety Razor Co.
1948   Toni Co.
1955   Paper Mate pens
1956   Harris Research Laboratories
1962   Soc. Francaise d'Appareillages et
            d'Instrument de Mesure S.A. (precision metalworking)
        Sterilon Corp. (disposable hospital supplies; sold 1971)
1967   Braun AG
1970   Autopoint Co. (writing instruments)
        North American Hair Goods

Table 25 (*continued*)

1971   Welcome Wagon, Ltd.
        S.T. Dupont
        Anant, S.A.
1972   Buxton, Inc.
1973   Jafra Cosmetics, Inc.
        Hydroponic Chemicals Co.
        Bassat S.A.
        Felicitas B.V.
1974   Jiffy Plastics
        Sunroid Pty., Ltd.
        Swiss Farms, Inc.
        Empress Products
        Day-Ease Home Products Corp.
1975   European gum and confectionary manufacturing
          company
1976   Athena Crafts, Inc.

International Business Machines Co.
1931   Filene-Finlay translator
1932   National Scale Corp.
1933   Electromatic Typewriter, Inc.
        "Radiotype" (device for transmitting graphic information)
1959   Peirce Wire Recorder Corp.
1964   Science Research Associates

Procter & Gamble
1929   National Cottonseed Products Corp.
1930   Thomas Hedley & Co., Ltd.
        James S. Kirk & Co.
1931   Sabates Sen Co.
        Portsmouth Cotton Oil Refining Co.
        Oil Seeds Crushing Co.
1935   J. Barcelou & Cie, Ltd.
1936   Cincinnati Soap Co.
1945   Spic & Span Products
1951   Buckeye Cellulose Corp.
1955   W.T. Young Foods, Inc. (peanut butter and salted peanuts)
1956   Nebraska Consolidated Mills Co.
        Hines-Park Foods, Inc.
        Duncan Hines Institute
1957   Charmin Paper Mills, Inc.
        Clorox Chemical Co. (divested)
1963   J.A. Folger & Co.
1965   Rei Werke A.G.
1972   Societa Generale Del Caffe

Table 25 (*continued*)

Pullman
1930	Standard Steel Car Co.
	Osgood-Bradley Co.
1944	M.W. Kellogg Co.
1951	Trailmobile Co.
1959	Swindel-Dressler
1965	Standard Steel Works, Inc.
1966	Trailmobile de Mexico, S.A.
	Canadian Trailmobile
1969	Berry Metal Co.
	Arthur W. Schmid Co.
1970	Aloe Coal Co. (sold 1974)
	F.C. Torkelson, Co.
	Societe Trailor
1971	Mahon Industrial Corp. (sold 1975)
	Marathon Service Co. (sold 1973)
	Penn Pocahontas Coal Co. (sold 1974)
	Societe Intercontinental des Containers
1972	Heat Research Corp.
1976	Transport Systems, Inc.
1978	First Greatwest Corp.

United Shoe Machinery (Emhart Corp.)
1956	A. Kimball Co. (sold 1960)
	K.J. Braun Engineering Co.
1962	Converter Corp.
1963	Safe-Pack Container Corp.
	Truelove & MacLean
	Dersal Corp.
1964	Rockwell Products Corp.
	Monitor Industries, Inc.
1965	Girder Process, Inc.
	Ammo Products Corp.
	Nylok Corp.
1966	Parker-Kalon
1967	U.S. Gear Corp.
	Warren Fastener Corp.
1968	Standard Tool Co.
	John Orme, Ltd.
	Farrel Corp.
1970	Spiras Systems, Inc.
	Bailey Co., Inc.
	Finch Paint & Chemical Co.
	Vibrac Corp.
	Schaeffer Magnetics, Inc.
	Crown-Metro, Inc.
	David Bridge & Co., Ltd.
	Red Sherman Associates, Inc.

Table 25 (*continued*)

1971	Icon Corp.
	S.A. Felton & Son Co.
	Krippendorf Kalculator Co.
	United-Lombard, Inc.
1976	Acquired by Emhart Industries

* Sources: *Moody's Industrials,* 1974-1978. Same volumes "Boeing," "Campbell Soup," "Coca-Cola," "Eastman Kodak," "International Business Machines Co.," "Procter & Gamble," "Pullman," "Gillette," "United Shoe Machinery."

Procter & Gamble has used acquisitions to broaden its product line. Between 1955 and 1957 it purchased Duncan Hines Cake Mixes, Charmin Paper Products, Big Top Peanut Butter, and Clorox. Its acquisitions have been household products that can be marketed through its current distribution network. With the exception of Clorox, Procter has bought companies only to establish a base for launching new products. The Charmin paper plant, for instance, was run down and involved no good will.[65]

The remaining firms—IBM, Kodak, and Boeing—have diversified very little. IBM and Kodak have not been faced with a situation of declining demand partially because of their own product innovation. Boeing does face an unstable demand, but the government has served to reduce some of this risk by providing a base of safe sales and profits.[66]

Our hypothesis was that if dominant firms diversify they will tend to move into related product areas. Generally, the basic technology of production proved less important in the acquisition than the marketing channels. In this respect acquisitions were in "related" product areas.

The stimulus to diversify came from two sources: a change in marketing methods or in the level of demand in the industry. It is not surprising that demand growth is important since dominant firms have a limited opportunity of increasing their market share otherwise. Only those firms that were able to control the growth of demand, or were insulated from changes in it, did not diversify.

Another reason for diversifying is to use it as a device for extending market power from one area to another. One acquisition which might fall into this category was Gillette's purchase of Braun AG, a producer of electric razors. An agreement with the Justice Department concerning this acquisition requires Gillette to divest itself of the part of the company which markets shavers in this country. Campbell Soup owns three fast-food chains, but antitrust laws prevent franchisers from forcing franchisees to buy supplies sold by the parent company. Exporting of dominance through acquisition does not appear to be a phenomenon of importance among this sample of firms.

Product type has an effect on the diversification of the firms only indirectly through its effect on demand. High technology firms have more opportunity and are more succesful at directing demand growth; those that declined were unable to do this. Firms producing branded consumer products in this sample are in lower growth industries and have diversified more extensively. It is relativey "easy" since they can simply add a product to a line being marketed through established channels.

Marketing Methods

Marketing methods are generally considered a product characteristic determining demand rather than an aspect of market conduct. There are, however, a variety of ways in which some products can be marketed. Dominant firms' decisions regarding distribution channels and marketing methods can affect the ability of other firms to enter the market. A practice of product leasing in an industry delays the receipt of payments and raises the capital necessary for a firm to do business. Alternatively, firms may choose to market their products as systems making it more difficult for firms producing only one component to compete. Because some aspects of marketing are discretionary and yet can affect the ability of other firms to compete, it will be examined here along with other non-price behavioral strategies.

Leasing was a common practice in the shoe machinery industry prior to the merger that resulted in the formation of United Shoe. United, nevertheless, continued the practice. It offered the option to buy on only a few machines, and its leases ran for ten years. Each United machine had to be used to full capacity if there was work available. Furthermore, the lease was subject to termination by United if it felt the leasee had more machinery than was needed. Return of a machine was accepted on payment of termination charges, deferred charges, and transportation. Each leasee had a right-of-deduction fund and received credits to it for a certain percentage of rents and royalties paid to United. This fund could be used against deferred payments when a machine was returned. It served to tie the many United machines together since credits to the fund received on one machine could be used against payments for another.[67]

In addition to tying machines together, leasing can be exclusionary because it tends to "tie" customers to producers. When a product is introduced, there is little incentive not to accept a lease if no replacement is available. The longer the term of the lease and the higher the penalties for cancellation, the more firmly customers are bound to the original leasor. This "tying" effect will be very important in industries such as computers in which the fringe must produce a product compatible with that of the dominant firm.

Like United Shoe, IBM did not create the pattern of leasing equipment in its industry; it was partially a carry-over from tabulating equipment. Prior to May 27, 1971, when IBM announced the Fixed Term Plan (FTP), its equipment was available for sale or on short-term lease, cancellable on 30 days notice. This was largely due to customer resistance to longer leases because of the rapidity of technological changes. Under the Fixed Term Plan, one- or two-year leases on certain disk, tape, and printer products were available. Substantial discounts on monthly rental rates were given—8% for one-year leases, and 16% for two-year leases—and extra use charges were eliminated. The effective price reduction under the two-year plan was 31% on disk products, 20% on tape products, and 30-35% on printers. Penalties for cancellation varied from two and one-half to five times the monthly rental, depending upon the length of the lease and time remaining under it at cancellation. CPU's were not placed under the Fixed Term Plan. In March 1972 a variation of the Fixed Term Plan, known as the Extended Term Plan, was announced, and in March 1973 a four-year lease on the System 370 virtual storage processors was offered. Many of IBM's peripheral competitors had been offering long-term leases, but after announcement of the Fixed Term Plan they also lowered lease prices. IBM estimates showed that the peripherals manufacturers' order rate was cut 50% after the Fixed Term Plan was offered. 90% of new IBM products placed were installed under the plan.[68]

The potential competitive effect of IBM's leases is two-fold. First, the leases represented substantial price cuts. Second, the length of the leases and penalties for cancellation were crucial. IBM studies indicated that cost would be reduced as a result of the leases because the turnover on equipment would be lower. However, IBM chose to selectively offer the leases. If cost reductions were a major consideration, it would probably have made them more widely available. Considering the pattern of competition in peripherals, that is, introduction of a product by IBM followed by introduction of competing products, the relationship of the length of the lease to the lag before competing products are available is crucial. Table 26 gives the chronology of product introduction by IBM and Telex and the number of months between their announcements and deliveries of products. Telex has reduced the time between IBM's delivery of products and its own delivery of products in some cases below 24 months. If a large number of customers have accepted long-term leases from IBM they will be unavailable as customers to the peripherals manufacturers. Even if the term of leases is shorter than the lag in deliveries there is a possible exclusionary effect due to the ties they create between manufacturer and customer.[69]

Both United Shoe's and IBM's leasing plans were tested in court. IBM's leases were upheld by the court of appeals as "ordinary marketing methods" while United's were judged violations of the Sherman Act.[70] The court differentiated the leases of IBM from those of United on the basis of their length and the fact that the option to buy did not exist under United's plans. The remedy in *United States vs. United Shoe Machinery Corp.* required that lease and sale terms be set such that leasing was not more advantageous than buying. The leases were to be no more than five years in duration and after one year they could be terminated. The district court decision in the *Telex vs. IBM*

Table 26. Chronology of Product Introductions in the Computer Industry*

Telex Product	Telex Announcement Date	Telex First Customer Shipment	IBM Product	IBM Announcement Date	IBM First Customer Shipment	Months Between IBM and Telex Announcements	Months Between IBM and Telex Deliveries
4700 Tape Drive	May 1966	Aug. 1966	729 Tape Drive	Jan. 1957	Aug. 1958	113	96
4800 Tape Drive	July 1967	Mar. 1968	2401 Tape Drive	Apr. 1964	May 1965	40	36
5311 Disk Drive	May 1969	Aug. 1969	2311 Disk Drive	Apr. 1964	Feb. 1965	62	55
5314 Disk Drive and Controller	May 1969	Apr. 1970	2314 Disk Drive and Controller	Apr. 1965	Mar. 1967	50	36
5420 (Mod 7) Tape Drive	May 1970	Dec. 1970	2420 (Mod 7) Tape Drive	Jan. 1968	Dec. 1968	29	24
5420 (Mod 5) Tape Drive	Aug. 1970	Feb. 1971	2420 (Mod 5) Tape Drive	Dec. 1968	Oct. 1969	20	16

6420/6803 Tape Drive and Controller	Dec. 1970	Nov. 1971	3420/3803 Tape Drive and Controller	Nov. 1970	Sept. 1971	1	2
5403/5821 Printer and Controller	Nov. 1970	Aug. 1971	1403N1/2821 Printer and Controller	Apr. 1964	June 1965	80	75
6360 Memory	Nov. 1971	Nov. 1972	3360 Memory	June 1970	Feb. 1971	19	22
6330/6830 Disk Drive and Controller	Nov. 1971	Oct. 1972	3330/3830 Disk Drive and Controller	June 1970	Aug. 1971	19	15
6345 Memory	Nov. 1971	Not yet delivered	3345 Memory	Sept. 1970	Nov. 1971	15	—
6721 Printer System	Aug. 1972	Not yet delivered	1403N1/2821 (Mod 2) Printer and Controller	Apr. 1964	June 1965	101	—

* Source: *Telex Corp. vs. International Business Machines Corp.*, 367 F. Supp. 1292.

case used the term of five years from the United remedy as a "judicially approved" length of lease and upheld IBM's leases since they were shorter. The opinion also noted that IBM's competitors had similar plans first and that firms had to have "room to move."[71]

Under ordinary circumstances both parties to a lease are constrained in some manner. For example, the leasor is constrained by the delay in the pattern of receipts. The leasee makes a commitment to use the machine for a certain period of time subject to cancellation penalties. In a competitive market situation all firms employing a given marketing device are constrained similarly. This was not the case in either the IBM or United leases. In an industry in which the technology is changing, the risk of obsolescence affects the purchase/lease decision. Theoretically the leasor bears this risk, but, to the extent that IBM controlled the rate of introduction of new products, it was able to escape it. United was able to impose full capacity clauses which would have been impossible for a firm without its market power. The legal status of leases has not yet been decided, however, when firms are constrained differently based upon their market power by an "ordinary" marketing method it is a candidate for an exclusionary practice.

The leasing practices of United and IBM illustrate how "exclusionary" behavior can have a broad definition. Other marketing practices are possible exclusionary devices. For example, systems introductions of products may hamper firms that produce only one component. Both IBM and Eastman Kodak have engaged in systems introductions of products. High technology products which have a number of components are particularly amenable to this. An exclusionary effect can result if firms with high market power in one "component" of a system introduce that product in conjunction with other components in which they do not have such market power. The case for exclusionary behavior in such instances is not clear-cut since it is easiest in products that are technology-intensive, but these same products may also require integration of parts to work best. Two examples of systems introductions will be examined below.

As a result of improvements in memory technology by competitors in the early 1970's, IBM accelerated its program for the development of semiconductor memories employing field effect transistor (FET) technology so that it could be delivered in 1973 rather than 1975. It employed a strategy of introducing upgraded 155 and 165 machines as new products rather than simply fitting them with memory enhancements. FET memory was placed inside the CPU in contrast to core memory which was in a separate box on the original 155 and 165 machines. The CPU itself was designed in such a way that attempts to attach separate memory units would require modifications in it.[72] In this instance, there is some evidence that it is technologically desirable to decrease the "distance" between memory and the central processing unit. There is also no doubt that IBM strengthened the "systems" aspects of its products by requiring a redesign of the CPU to attach separate memory.

Development of the line of Kodak Instamatic cameras took ten years during which the project was kept a secret. The key feature of this camera system was a cartridge-loading film. Successful development required a cartridge which was both inexpensive and stable. To be all-purpose, the camera had to take black-and-white film plus three kinds of color film. All of these films had to be adjusted so that they worked at the same speed. Because amateurs have a tendency to under-expose film, a high-speed, ASA64, was chosen. This speed was the norm for Kodak black-and-white film. Kodachrome II was brought up from ASA25 and Kodacolor and Ektachrome were brought up from ASA32. The use of a high-speed film also allowed a less expensive plastic lens to be used in the camera.[73] On February 28, 1963, Kodak conducted a simultaneous worldwide introduction.

In both cases a dominant firm employed a systems introduction or integration of products. The competitive implications depend upon the technological necessity of the integration or development. In the introduction of the Kodak Instamatic, a case can be made on technological grounds for the manner of introduction. The camera could only operate at one shutter speed, so film speed was adjusted. The choice of a high speed made possible the use of a cheap plastic lens in the camera. Obviously the camera was not useful if film was not available, hence the worldwide introduction of the product. In contrast, the manner in which IBM introduced FET memory was not technologically determined. In particular, the design of the CPU so that logic modifications would be required for memory attachments implies exclusionary tactics.

To the extent that technology determines the competitive character of a systems introduction, it must be judged on a case-by-case basis. However, some firms exhibit a consistent pattern of introductions of collateral equipment. Table 27 lists other instances of systems of products introduced by Kodak. In movie cameras Kodak does not have as substantial market power as in still cameras. The competitive effect of a systems introduction is obviously less. The introduction of the Pocket Instamatic 110 camera is similar to that of the earlier Instamatic camera. Development of the camera and film are uniquely related, and Kodak's market power in film assures that it is the only firm capable of performing the task.

While technology is one factor that determines the competitive character of a systems introduction, the system aspects of a product, in turn, can affect the speed of technical change. If two interrelated products are developed together by one firm, more technical change may result than if it must wait upon action by others. For example, more new products may result if Kodak is developing both film and cameras. The technological options for a dominant firm producing inter-related products may thus be greater, but it will not necessarily exercise them unless "pushed" by competitors. IBM accelerated its development program in memory only after peripheral competitors had made improvements.

Table 27.   Introductions of Collateral Equipment by Eastman Kodak*

1963	Instamatic camera and cartridge film
1965	Super 8 movie film, cameras, and projectors
1971	X-L movie camera, Ektachrome film (40 and 60), and Ektachrome Autoprocessor. Photographic paper and a three-step finishing process
1972	Pocket Instamatic 110 camera, Kodacolor II film in that format, photofinishing equipment, and photofinishing process.

*   Sources: "Competitors attack Kodak's dominance." *Business Week,* 26 May 1973, pp. 29-30; *Berkey Photo, Inc. vs. Eastman Kodak Co.,* 457 F. Supp. 404 (1978).

Manipulation of marketing methods is a behavioral strategy more common among producers of high technology products. Obviously, leasing is not practical for producers of branded consumer products. They can, however, engage in systems introductions of products. Gillette produces both razors and blades, or shaving "systems." Other firms make cartridges that fit Gillette's razors' handles, but Gillette cartridges do not fit the handles of other producers. This is the only instance of a systems approach to marketing observed among the branded consumer products examined here.

Summary and Conclusions

As a competitive device, non-price policies were used extensively by this sample of firms. In many cases they were employed in lieu of price policies. There were several instances in which firms introduced new products rather than cut prices. More often, firms simply altered old products or introduced new ones as a competitive device. Marketing devices, such as leasing or systems introductions of products, proved to be another way in which firms could alter the "products," at least in the eyes of the consumer.

Other non-price behavioral attributes of firms include their research and development policies and their investment policies. One of the justifications often offered for high market power is that firms which possess it are more likely to be innovators, perhaps because of economies of scale in R&D. The majority of our information for this sample dealt with product innovations. In this area, the dominant firms' innovations did not justify their market share. We had little information on process innovations. Dominant firms might be expected to have a higher level of research effort in this area since, for example, any cost reduction would be applied to a high volume of output. More data on process innovations might strengthen the case for dominance.

The final behaviors that we examined were the firms' policies related to vertical integration and diversification. In general, they tended to integrate vertically either to increase their control over the quality of inputs or to exercise their market power as a large buyer. Diversification policies were most closely related to demand conditions in the industries; firms in low growth industries tended to diversify. There was no evidence of the exporting of market power by acquisition.

Product type affected the non-price policies available to the different firms. All of the producers of branded consumer goods engaged in proliferation strategies of some sort, while producers of high technology items relied on product changes or marketing techniques as competitive devices. In addition, high technology producers tend to be less diversified since they have an opportunity to affect demand growth through their product policies rather than resorting to diversification.

Non-price behavior in and of itself is only of academic interest. It is of importance because it shapes the evolving market structure. The feedbacks from non-price conduct to structure will be examined in chapter 6.

6

Feedbacks from Conduct to Structure

In the preceding chapter we reviewed the non-price policies that dominant firms used as competitive devices. Our discussion followed the traditional paradigm of industrial organization economics in which structure, in this case the dominant firm structure, led to certain types of behavior. Possible interactions between conduct and structure were ignored. In this chapter we broaden our approach to include possible feedbacks from conduct to structure. Firm price and non-price policies are not only determinants of performance but also determinants of structural factors such as the height of barriers to entry and the cost structure of the industry. The existence of these feedbacks implies that firms having discretionary power with respect to conduct also have the power to affect the way in which market structure evolves. Because we are interested in the persistence of dominant firms, their ability to determine structure through conduct is of particular importance.

Conduct may affect market structure both directly and indirectly. It may determine the height of entry barriers and the cost structure as mentioned earlier, or it may alter the degree of product differentiation and vertical integration. All of these are actual characteristics of market structure. Indirectly, conduct can alter structure by affecting the basic conditions of supply and demand which generate structure. Firm policies that alter the rate of growth of demand and the underlying product technology also have an effect on structure.

In this chapter we shall be concerned with both the direct and the indirect effects of conduct on structure. They will be examined in the first two sections respectively. The last section will contain a summary and conclusions.

Direct Effects of Conduct on Market Structure

"Market structure" is sometimes used to denote the number of buyers and sellers in a market. Most textbooks, however, define market structure to include the degree of product differentiation, the height of barriers to entry, and the general cost structure of the industry. Hence the non-price behavior of dominant firms in the form of their product strategies, R&D policies, investment decisions, and integration strategies can potentially affect these other structural characteristics. In the discussion below, we shall emphasize the direct effects of conduct by dominant firms on barriers to entry, the cost structure, and the degree of product differentiation. Dominant firm conduct, apart from predation, rarely affects the number of sellers directly but instead operates through an alteration in these other "structural" characteristics.

Barriers to Entry

Anything that makes entry unprofitable or difficult can be classified as a barrier to entry. The most frequently discussed barriers are technical; that is, economies of scale. They will not be examined here unless they are the direct consequence of the conduct of a dominant firm. Aside from technical barriers related to differential access to methods of production, firms trying to enter a market may have difficulty using standard marketing channels or manufacturing a product that is compatible with that of dominant firms in their markets.

The most important source of entry barriers among dominant firms' non-price strategies is their product policies. An important consequence of product proliferation, the selling of a large number of differentiated products by a dominant firm, is its effect on the ease and profitability of entry. In consumer goods, product proliferation strategies can reduce the amount of shelf space available to an entrant if it is allocated by model, variety, or brand, but if shelf space is allocated by producer this will not be the case. Firms trying to enter or expand may find it more difficult to convince retailers to carry their product if the retailers already have a large number of models/varieties/brands to offer customers. If the same shelf space is held by five or six brands or models instead of one, retailers might be hesitant to add a new product, especially if it meant dropping a product they currently carry.

A more subtle barrier is erected by product proliferation strategies if consumer choice of products is random among brands. In that event, the more facings of a product a company has, the more likely one of its products will be purchased. This idea is in direct conflict with traditional theories of consumers as rational, utility maximizing beings. These theories, however, assume consumers have perfect knowledge and search is costless while in reality neither of these conditions are met. The time costs alone of choosing among many competing varieties or brands may dictate a random selection.

Other entry deterring effects of brand proliferation are examined by Richard Schmalensee in his study of the breakfast cereal industry.[1] Using a spatial competition framework with the assumption that it is costly to reposition brands in the space of consumer perceptions, he argues that established brands may earn excess profits while entry remains unattractive. If established firms crowd the economic space prior to the threat of entry, it serves as a deterrent to entrants who assume the brands cannot or will not be moved. An alternative behavior on the part of entrants is to imitate established brands, but proliferation policies also serve to deter entry in this form. The more brands have been proliferated, the smaller is the market share an imitator can hope to capture.

If product proliferation becomes the accepted mode of competition, it can also result in capital barriers to entry. New entrants may find it difficult to raise the funds necessary to launch a panel of products rather than one or two. Brand proliferation will result in higher barriers than the other types of product proliferation to the extent that it costs more to launch a new brand than to launch an additional model or variety.

When will product proliferation be an effective deterrent strategy for a dominant firm? The entry deterring effects based upon a shelf space constraint depend upon the method of marketing common in the industry and the set of assumptions about the nature of consumer choice. The effects described by Schmalensee depend upon the validity of his assumptions: the existence of costs to reposition brands, the localized nature of rivalry such that any actions have effects on a limited number of brands, increasing returns within a brand, and relatively static demand. These conditions were found most often among the branded consumer products, and all of the firms of this product type employed product proliferation in some form. The nature of demand in the industries is crucial to the continuing success of product proliferation in deterring entry or expansion by the fringe. The controversy over phosphates in detergents provided the opportunity for entry by washing soda manufacturers. Likewise, the change in "tastes" in soft drinks has allowed the fringe to expand through introduction of diet drinks and fruit flavored drinks. By and large, demand in branded products industries has proven stable, and product proliferation strategies continue to be an important device for maintaining dominance.

Firm policies with regard to product changes can create barriers if the fringe must produce compatible products. This was one of IBM's strategies with regard to the plug compatible peripheral manufacturers which we examined in the previous chaper. Procter also used it to direct attention away from a product in which it did not have a leading share in the Dash and Salvo incident examined in chapter 5.

Leasing, as a marketing method, has a two-fold effect on the ease of entry. First, it creates a capital barrier as a result of the delay of receipt of payments. Second, it tends to create manufacturer-customer ties which other firms may have difficulty breaking. Both IBM and United Shoe leased some of their products. In United Shoe's case, it was an important support of its market power.

A final way in which firms can create barriers to entry through non-price strategies is by their investment in capacity whether it be in the form of plant and equipment, bottler networks, or advertising. Investments in advertising will be discussed below in the section on product differentiation. Although product differentiation is a source of barriers to entry, it is also an important characteristic of market structure and will be discussed separately.

There was little evidence in the dominant firms studied here of the use of plant capacity to deter entry. Soft drink firms do require a bottler network but this is a consequence of technology rather than being imposed by a dominant firm's decision. In Douglas Aircraft's case, there was negative evidence that firms use capacity to preserve their market position.

Two Examples of Entry into Dominant Firm Markets

So far we have identified several discretionary firm actions which tend to make entry difficult. Another way to gain insight into the generation of barriers to entry through firm conduct is to study attempted entry in dominant firm industries. Entry into the razor blade and detergent markets will be examined below. In both instances the firms were outsiders but possessed significant product innovations. The difficulty they had entering helps explain the persistence of market power on the part of dominant firms.

Wilkinson stainless steel blades.   Stainless steel razor blades had been marketed by Gillette as early as 1930. Although they lasted longer than carbon steel blades, they did not give as good a shave. In the process of adding chromium to carbon to produce stainless steel, large particles called carbides are formed. When stainless steel is sharpened, these particles rip off leaving an irregular edge. The solution is to coat the edge making it more even. In March 1962 Wilkinson Sword began marketing a coated chromium steel blade in the United States. Schick Safety Razor and American Safety Razor entered in early 1963.[2] Gillette had planned to market such a blade in mid-1964. It speeded up development and entered in September 1963. Once in the market, Gillette moved rapidly. It gave away blades and within three months had acquired fifty percent of the market.[3] Wilkinson was not successful in displacing Gillette for three reasons. Its first problem was the distribution channels it used. When Wilkinson entered the United States market, it began by placing blades in hardware stores and garden shops—the distribution network for its line of garden tools. The blades were well received, and as other stores sought to sell them Wilkinson established a system of authorized dealers. In order to carry the blades, a retailer also had to carry the garden tools. The blades were thus marketed outside usual channels. This problem notwithstanding, Wilkinson had insufficient capacity to "flood" the market and establish themselves prior to Gillette's entry.[4] Finally, when Wilkinson came out with its blade, Gillette claimed that it had a key patent on the process used to coat the blade. Rather than pursuing the dispute in court, Wilkinson agreed to pay Gillette a 2% royalty on United States' sales and a 4.5% royalty on sales elsewhere.[5] A combination of delays due to lawsuits, insufficient capacity, and unwise distribution allowed Gillette to regain its position. The changing fortunes of Gillette, as reflected in its market share, are detailed in table 28.

Table 28.   Market Shares in Razor Blades, 1946-1972*

	1946	1962	1963	1964	1965	1972
Gillette	40%	70%	69%	60%	56%	60%
Schick			18	22	22	20
American Safety Razor			11	16	17	10
Wilkinson			**	**	2	10
Others			2	2	3	

* Sources: Walter Guzzardi, Jr. "Gillette Faces the Stainless-Steel Dragon." *Fortune* 68 (July 1963): 159; Patrick J. Kelly. "They're Creeping Up on Giant Gillette." *Printers' Ink* 291 (June 11, 1965): 50; William M. Carley. "Gillette, Often Criticized by Marketing Men as Stodgy, Gets More Lively—and Profitable." *Wall Street Journal*, Eastern edition, 24 October 1972, p. 13.
** Not reported separately.

Monsanto's All.   In the early 1940's Westinghouse developed a front-loading automatic washing machine whose cleaning action was impeded by excess suds. It subsequently asked Monsanto to develop a synthetic detergent that would wash well without foam. Monsanto was successful and approached all of the big three soap makers to market the product. Each, in turn, refused, feeling demand was too limited. Consequently, Monsanto formed a company, Detergents, Inc., to market and promote the detergent as a product that could be used in any washer. When demand grew so large that Detergents, Inc. could not handle it, Monsanto re-acquired the company.[6]

Initially, Monsanto did well with the product. All was sold by appliance dealers, then department stores. Distribution through grocery and hardware stores was begun in 1951. Monsanto began the practice of packing its product in washers and paying premiums to appliance dealers and service personnel to demonstrate All.[7] Its good fortunes continued until Procter & Gamble discovered the low-suds market.

In 1954 Dash was introduced by Procter & Gamble. All's market share dropped from 97.4% in 1954 to 54.5% in 1957, while Dash's rose to 31.2%. Monsanto, which had relied extensively on free samples as a promotion device, moved heavily into media expenditures. From $5,000,000 in 1953 they rose to $12,000,000 in 1955, while case sales rose from 2,389,000 to 4,421,000. Table 30 presents the advertising and promotion expenses per case for various products. Monsanto's per case costs were higher than those of other established products such as Tide, Cheer, and Surf, but less than what Procter was willing to spend on its new product, Dash.[8]

Table 29.   Market Shares of Low-Sudsing Detergent
Brands, 1954-1960*,**

	All	Ad	Dash
	Monsanto Chemical and Lever Brothers[a]	Colgate-Palmolive	Procter & Gamble
1954	97.4%	b	2.6%
1955	79.2	14.3%	6.5
1956	55.3	18.2	26.5
1957	54.5	14.3	31.2
1958	51.7	14.7	33.6
1959	46.4	18.5	35.1
1960	44.9	13.4	41.7

* Source: Lawrence Bernard. "Couldn't Compete Without All, Says Lever President." Reprinted with permission from the January 21, 1963 issue of *Advertising Age.* Copyright 1963 by Crain Communications, Inc., p. 77.
** Note: Figures are on a case basis. Neilson Food Store data was adjusted to all-outlet basis by Lever Projection factors.
a. Lever marketed All subsequent to 22 May 1957.
b. Not marketed.

By 1955 Monsanto had lost $2,900,000 on All—largely due to ad expenditures. In addition, Procter began to offer automatic washing machine manufacturers free advertising if they would pack Procter products.[9] In March of 1956, Monsanto began looking for a buyer for All. It discussed sale of the product with General Foods, Armour & Co., and Purex before approaching Lever in January 1957. On May 22, 1957 an agreement with Lever was concluded.

Monsanto failed with All for several reasons. It sold All through food brokers, the result being that 12-13% of net sales receipts were allocated to selling expenses. At one point it even tried to find another consumer product over which to spread promotion expenditures. For firms such as Procter & Gamble which have their own sales force, selling costs were only 3% of receipts. Monsanto was unable to get volume discounts on television ads, and partly because of inexperience it concentrated too much advertising in newspapers. Meanwhile, Procter & Gamble effectively marketed Dash by means of samples and coupons. Finally, at the time Monsanto owned the product there were deficiencies in it: All had a tendency to cake on the shelf, and in cities with bad air pollution it turned white cloth green. Monsanto was unwilling to spend the amount required to rectify these problems.

Lever, on the other hand, was successful with All. Sales increased from $30 million in 1956 to $44 million in 1959, but Lever was using only half the advertising budget Monsanto had used in 1956. Lever also improved the deficiencies in the product.[11] Its ad expenditures per case were even lower than Dash's as indicated in table 31.

Table 30. Advertising and Promotion Expense, per Case Cost,
1954-1957*,**

	Advertising and Promotion Expenditures (000 Omitted)	Case Sales (000 Omitted)	Advertising and Promotion Cost per Case
1954			
Lever			
Rinso Blue	$ 3.558	1.460	$ 2.437
Surf	6.483	3.794	1.709
P&G			
Tide	15.000	22.483	.667
Cheer	11.000	9.468	1.162
Dash	500	90	5.556
Monsanto			
All	7.590	3.396	2.235
1955			
Lever			
Rinso Blue	$10.614	3.145	$ 3.375
Surf	4.300	2.786	1.543
P&G			
Tide	16.000	23.558	.679
Cheer	9.000	9.786	.920
Dash	2.000	366	5.472
Monsanto			
All	12.194	4.421	2.758
1956			
Lever			
Rinso Blue	$ 5.574	3.462	$ 1.610
Surf	2.812	2.357	1.193
P&G			
Tide	16.000	24.478	.647
Cheer	10.000	9.726	1.028
Dash	14.000	2.080	6.731
Monsanto			
All	8.870	4.331	2.048
1957			
Lever			
Rinso Blue	$ 5.094	3.185	$ 1.599
Surf	2.602	1.912	1.361
All (7 months)	4.250	2.759	1.540

Table 30 (*continued*)

	Advertising and Promotion Expenditures (000 Omitted)	Case Sales (000 Omitted)	Advertising and Promotion Cost per Case
P&G			
Tide	16.000	25.480	.628
Cheer	9.000	10.047	.896
Dash	5.000	2.604	1.920
Monsanto			
All (5 months)	2.465	1.784	1.382

* Source: Lawrence Bernard. "Lever Defense: It Was All or Nothing at All." Reprinted with permission from the January 28, 1963 issue of *Advertising Age*. Copyright 1963 by Crain Communications, Inc., p. 98.

** Note: Advertising and promotion figures direct from companies; case sales Nielson estimates.

Table 31. Per Case Advertising Expenditures for All and Dash, 1958-1962*

	1958	1959	1960	1961	1962
Lever: All	$1.36	$1.12	$1.11	$1.09	$1.30
P & G: Dash**	1.48	1.27	1.36	1.37	1.49

* Source: Lawrence Bernard. "Lever Defense: It Was All or Nothing at All." Reprinted with permission from the January 28, 1963 issue of *Advertising Age*. Copyright 1963 by Crain Communications, Inc., p. 60.

** Figures for Procter & Gamble are their estimates.

In both instances firms outside the industry found entry difficult despite product innovations. Wilkinson initially tried to use different distribution channels and suffered from that. Monsanto found the promotion costs of one product too high. These new firms did not find themselves deterred by product loyalty for "old" products. Instead, old firms seem to develop intangible capital related to marketing techniques and distribution channels. This capital, along with substantial production capacity, enables dominant firms to saturate a product type once they begin its production. Product loyalty enters to the extent that new entrants do not have time to develop a strong brand preference before established firms can begin production. If an innovation in a consumer product proved patentable this might not be the case.

To what extent did conduct of established firms actually affect entry? Wilkinson's problems were as much the result of its own business decisions as the actions of Gillette, although it was hindered by Gillette's law suit. In Monsanto's case, the established pattern of product proliferation in the industry meant that it was at a disadvantage relative to other firms in terms of selling expenses. This barrier to entry was the result of a distribution system that put a producer of a single product at a disadvantage relative to one with many products. The dominant firm established the pattern of multiproduct production that gave it an advantage in this respect. Monsanto's other problems stemmed from its own inexperience regarding distribution channels and promotion methods in the detergent industry which may be described as an industry specific, managerial capital barrier.

Cost Structure

The technology of production itself is one of the most important determinants of an industry's cost structure. One way that firms can alter it through their conduct is by process innovation, but evidence related to such innovation is difficult to obtain. In this sample, Kodak is the best example of a firm that has altered its cost structure through process innovations. George Eastman established cost reducing practices as part of company policy, and efforts to keep costs at a minimum are part of Kodak's on-going quality control program.

Firms may also alter their cost structure by adding other products to their line. The phrase "economies of scope" was coined by Panzer and Willig to describe situations in which the joint production of two or more goods is less than the sum of the costs of their production separately.[12] Economies of scope arise when an input can be utilized in the production of more than one good without complete congestion. The sales network of firms may be one such input. Recall the attempt by Monsanto to enter the detergent industry. It was forced to sell through food brokers and warehouses while firms such as Procter had their own sales force. Gillette and Campbell also jointly produce and market a number of products with the likelihood that they experience similar effects, although we have no explicit evidence in this regard. Economies of scope, particularly if they arise in marketing, may follow from a firm's diversification strategy as well as from its product strategies. Those acquisitions by dominant firms that were most successful were the ones involving products within established marketing channels.

Baumol and Fischer have done related work on multiproduct technology. In a recent paper they report the findings of a study of the conditions under which various market structures evolve.[13] Their analysis starts with a given product vector and determines the cost-minimizing number of firms for that vector. They emphasize that the way in which the industry is defined has an effect on the range of firm sizes likely to evolve. The products generally produced by firms in a multiproduct industry are either substitutes in production or substitutes in consumption. Baumol and Fischer demonstrate that when the capital in a multiproduct industry is specialized, that is, little equipment is used in the production of more than one output, a considerable range in firm size is possible. This is most likely to occur when products are substitutes in consumption. Under these circumstances, the industry may contain several large firms supplying a broad range of products and a number of small enterprises that are more specialized. Several of the firms in this sample make products that are substitutes in consumption. Procter produces a variety of cleaning agents, Gillette produces different styles of shaving devices, and IBM produces many sizes of computers. In each case there are small firms in the industry producing specialized products as well as the dominant firm which produces a wider range of items.

Baumol and Fischer's analysis was based upon the "equilibrium" concept of minimization of total cost of industry output, in other words, they hypothesized that through mergers and divisions of firms, market structure would tend to that which minimizes costs. Their analysis suggests that, given the product mix of the industry and independence of capital equipment, the dominant firm market structure would be that which minimizes industry cost. They do not discuss how the product mix is chosen. The present study suggests that the dominant firm is able to control this variable, and thus indirectly it may affect the cost structure of the industry.

Vertical integration is another device for altering an industry's cost structure. Eastman Kodak is extensively integrated both forward and backward. One reason George Eastman gave for beginning this policy was to lower costs. Campbell Soup and IBM are also vertically integrated. IBM estimated that it had 15% lower costs as a result of in-house production of circuits used in tape drives.[14]

Although the evidence is scanty, the effects of dominant firm actions on the cost structure of their industries seem to be important in the maintenance of their market power. The research by Panzar, Willig, Baumol, and Fischer suggests that product policies are important competitive devices that determine the cost structure.

Product Differentiation

Another aspect of market structure is the degree to which the offerings of rival producers are differentiated from each other. The scope for possible product differentiation is limited only by the number of dimensions of the product. It can be based on differences in location, service, quality, or image.

In terms of firm behavior that affects product differentiation, advertising policies come most readily to mind and are associated with image differences, but marketing methods, such as leasing or systems introductions of products, may serve the same purpose. Leasing, which both IBM and United Shoe employed, creates ties between customer and manufacturer. Customers become accustomed to dealing with one company and are reluctant to switch. Leasing may differentiate a product both on the grounds of image and the actual quality of the product. It helps firms like IBM emphasize that they are selling a service rather than just a machine.

Systems introductions may leave the impression in the minds of consumers that a component produced by someone else will not work as well. Kodak touted the 110 camera and Kodacolor II film as the "film that was made for the camera that was made for the film."[15] IBM, which has employed systems introductions of products, also provides consulting and programming assistance to its customers and this further distinguishes them.

"Quality" was an important source of product loyalty in explaining the origin of this sample's dominance; it remains an important factor in the differentiation of their products. It is emphasized most by firms producing branded consumer products, but among the firms making high-technology products, Kodak has also advertised the quality and reliability of its products. Campbell Soup and Coke, the two producers of food products, employed mixtures of quality and image differentiation. In addition to the taste aspects of their products, their advertising suggests a life style, hence the "Campbell life" and "Coke adds life" campaigns.

Vertical integration contributes to product differentiation through an increase in the control of inputs. Kodak used this tactic. Campbell specified characteristics of inputs to accomplish the same thing rather than resorting to integration.

Perhaps the most subtle form of product differentiation is that which a dominant position itself renders. The companies and their products become synonymous.

> Such is the consumer magic of the Kodak name and its ubiquitous yellow box, that yellow has come to be one of the favorite box colors of several photo competitors. When Technicolor Corp. of America plunged into amateur 8mm film in 1961, it debated over the color of its box and decided it could not *afford* to market in a different-colored box. Dynacolor Corp., yet another new Kodak competitor in color film, also markets in a yellow-tone box. Says Dynacolor Vice President Eldon Bauer: "to the typical American the yellow box is synonymous with photography."[16]

Gillette and IBM have also become associated with their products to such an extent that other firms are forced to produce compatible products.

Product differentiation itself is not necessarily an undesirable characteristic of a market structure. The welfare implications vary by method of differentiation. Dominant firms may differentiate themselves simply by producing a product of high quality, and as a result they may be able to charge a price premium for it.

Summary of the Direct Effects of Conduct on Structure

To what extent did firm conduct determine or direct the evolving market structure? In four instances it had a substantial effect. Procter & Gamble's policy of brand proliferation and its wide product line yield economies in distribution. One potential entrant found this barrier insurmountable. IBM's marketing methods, both leasing and systems introductions, serve to tie customers to it, but in the long-run its policies with regard to product change are probably more important. In the experiences of Coca-Cola and United Shoe, conduct which the firms failed to undertake or were prevented from undertaking led to a decline in their market power. Coca-Cola let its market position slip before it recognized the value of additional brands/varieties/models. United Shoe was forced to change the nature of its leases which severed some of the manufacturer-customer ties and aided the development of a second-hand market.

In the cases of Kodak, Gillette, and Campbell, firm conduct has altered the way market structure evolved but other indirect effects to be discussed below are probably more important in terms of explaining their persistence. Eastman Kodak's vertical integration affected the cost structure of the photographic industry and also the level of product differentiation through quality. Gillette and Campbell Soup both engaged in forms of product proliferation that affected the ability of other firms to compete. To fully understand the persistence of Kodak, Gillette, and Campbell, we must examine the effect their conduct had on the basic conditions of supply and demand in their industries.

Indirect Effects of Conduct on Market Structure

Basic conditions of supply and demand generate a market structure which in turn generates firm conduct in the usual paradigm of industrial organization analysis. In the preceding section we examined the direct feedbacks from conduct to structure, but conduct can indirectly affect structure by altering the basic supply and demand conditions. For example, firm conduct through R&D policies affects product technology and durability or though product strategies affects the rate of growth of demand. Below we shall examine the influences of firm behavior on the rate of growth of demand, the underlying product technology, and product characteristics such as standardization and durability. These influences are of interest, however, only insofar as they generate market structure. Thus we shall also examine how they determine the evolving dominant firm structure.

Rate of Growth of Demand

By definition, a dominant firm has little room to expand. It is of necessity forced to move into other areas, and one way is through introduction of new products and creation of a demand for them. The success of both Campbell Soup and Procter & Gamble has been attributed to this.

Despite secrecy surrounding Campbell's formulas, the real secret seems to be that it actually invents the market it dominates. "We produce things consumers like once they try them," says Murphy [Campbell president]. In other words, nobody knows they want the products Campbell brings to market until a sales pitch is put behind them.[17]

[Procter's] research and development program is aimed not at giving consumers what they want, but rather at giving consumers what they will want or should want.[8]

Establishment and maintenance of dominance in a dynamic world requires that firms concern themselves with the demand for their products. It was the strategy used in the past by Gillette when it built a demand for home-shaving. George Eastman employed it when professional photographers displayed little interest in his inventions:

When we started out with our scheme of film photography, we expected that everybody that used glass plates would take up films, but we found that the number that did this was relatively small and in order to make a large business we would have to reach the general public and create a new class of patrons.[19]

Kodak's enduring market power is also the result of the effect of its products on demand. The novelty of a camera is crucial for amateur photographers, and as cameras age they buy less and less film. Photographic products, including cameras, have shown peak marketability in periods of less than five years.

New products are essential in maintaining user interest in photography. The amateur consumer market is highly responsive to technical innovations which improve the performance, convenience and reliability of moderately priced cameras and accessories.[20]

Kodak's new product introductions, such as the Super 8 movie camera and the Instamatic, created new markets for series of related equipment. Even Kodak's competitors acknowledge its effect on demand.

"Prior to Kodak's introduction of the Instamatic," says Bell & Howell's Peter Peterson, "the industry had been characterized by little if any growth..."[21]

Kodak's earnings as depicted in figure 4 reveal the effect of its innovations.

Similarly, IBM helped create the demand for computers. The IBM 650 was offered free to any university offering courses using that machine in the 1950's, and educational discounts were offered on other machines to encourage the use of computers—IBM computers in particular.[22] IBM's new product introductions, such as the 4300 series, continue to expand demand by increasing the size of the consumer population for which computers are practical.

The number of potential consumers of a product may be limited as in the case of Gillette. It has therefore focused on increasing the demand for a higher

Figure 4.   Annual Percentage Change in Earnings of Eastman Kodak
and New Product Introductions*

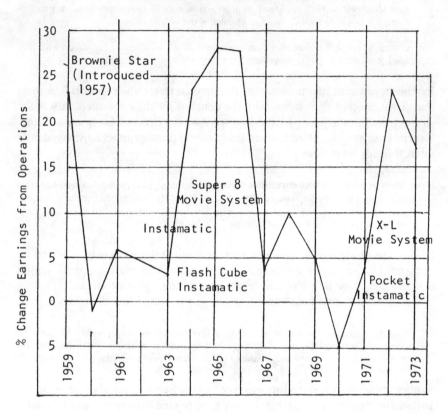

*   Source: Brenda Lee Landry, White, Weld & Co. Cited in "The Blurry Picture at Eastman Kodak." *Forbes* 114(15 September 1974): 86.

quality product. The initial effect of the invention of the safety razor was to
shift the underlying demand curve for "shaves" to the right. Further shifts in
demand can result from increases in the number of people who shave and from
increases in their number of shaves. The possibilities of increasing demand by
these methods are limited with the exception of an increase in the frequency
with which women shave. The other possible strategy is to alter the demand for
quality, that is, to convince people to trade up to a product that offers a "closer,
more comfortable" shave. This is the strategy that Gillette has been pursuing. It
has introduced both premium versions of existing blades and new shaving
systems. While the initial effect of these product introductions is on demand, a
secondary effect is on the other competitors in the industry. Gillette did not
produce a single-edge razor, and the Techmatic was designed to woo these

consumers.[23] Rather than competing in a single-edge market, Gillette opted to alter the nature of competition.

The success of Gillette's product strategies, particularly those related to altering demand, is constrained by the buying patterns in its market. The Super Blue blade did not catch on quickly with consumers and the theory at Gillette is that men do not move rapidly to try new products.[24] Also Gillette executives estimate that forty-five percent of blade purchases are made by women.[25] Whenever the purchasers and ultimate consumers do not coincide, a strategy based upon altering demand through new products is less likely to be successful.

At this point we have noted that those dominant firms that have persisted have successfully directed demand growth, but what of those that declined? Coca-Cola did not move aggressively to market new brands or varieties of soft drinks, a potential method of increasing the rate of growth of demand. Table 32 presents data on the percentage growth rates of various soft drink flavors. The diet market recently has shown the highest growth rates and within that category lemon-lime and cherry flavored drinks have out-paced colas. The cola market itself has been declining in importance in the last fifteen years relative to other flavor categories. Coke's strength has always been in the cola market; by neglecting other flavors it has placed itself in the low-growth segment of the soft drink industry. In addition, Coke's strength has been in the fountain rather than the take-home trade, but take-home now accounts for the majority of soft drink sales. Chain supermarkets, grocery stores, and other retail outlets accounted for sixty percent of soft drink sales in 1971 as indicated in table 33. The changing nature of the underlying demand indicates the direction of successful product strategy. Coca-Cola is only now moving away from cola flavors and more actively pursuing the take-home trade.

A general decline in demand is an important cause of the lack of persistence of a dominant firm. Neither United Shoe nor Pullman directed the growth of demand in their industries. Rather, a general decline in demand led to waning of their market power.

If a product is a radically new form of good or way of delivering a service, there is no existing demand, and the firm must create it. But the maintenance of dominance requires that firms continue the same strategy. Those firms that declined were by and large in low or slow growth industries and made no efforts to extend demand. Gillette, which is not in a rapidly growing market, has been able to sustain its position through improvements in the "quality" of shaving. All of the currently dominant firms have endeavored to increase demand or to create a demand for a flow of new products. The only exception is Boeing. It is in an unusual position since it faces a small number of buyers and the demand for its goods is derived from the demand for transportation services.

Innovation is a means by which firms may enter and thus increase the number of market participants, or it may be a device in the hands of dominant

Table 32.   Market Growth in the Soft Drink Industry,
1975-1977*,**, ***

	1975	1976	1977
By Type			
Regular	(3.0)	8.3	7.0
Diet	14.0	22.0	13.0
By Flavor			
Regular Cola	(2.0)	9.5	7.0
Regular Lemon-Lime	(5.3)	7.7	7.0
Regular Pepper and Mr. Pibb	6.3	14.0	14.0
Diet Cola	11.0	19.0	16.0
Diet Lemon-Lime	40.0	26.4	6.0
Diet Pepper	30.7	30.0	17.0
Total Market	(0.9)	10.0	8.0

*   Percent.
**   Source: Joseph C. Frazzano. "Soft Drink Brand and Flavor Shares." *Beverage World* 97 (April 1978): 18.
***   Note: Negative growth rates are in parentheses.

Table 33.   Major End Markets and Estimated Shares of Sales in the Soft
Drink Industry, 1971*

End Market	Percent of Total
Chain supermarkets	35
Grocery and convenience stores	20
Restaurants and bars	15
Service stations	12
Recreational outlets	7
Other "on-premise" outlets	6
Other retail outlets	5

*   Source: Predicasts, Inc. and Softdrinks. Cited in U.S. Congress, Senate, Subcommittee on Antitrust and Monopoly Hearings, *Exclusive Territorial Allocation Legislation,* 92nd Congress, 2d Session, August 8-10, September 12 and 14, 1972. Washington, D.C.: U.S. Government Printing Office, 1973, p. 62.

firms for hindering the ability of firms to compete. The dominant firms' lack of product change has facilitated entry more often than their active innovation has hindered it. United Shoe, Pullman, and Coke were all slow to innovate. More important in terms of sustaining the market structure has been a series of small product changes, (Gillette, Eastman Kodak, IBM), brand introductions (Procter & Gamble) and variety introductions (Campbell).

Product Characteristics/Standardization

Firm conduct can alter the basic supply conditions of the industry as well as the basic demand conditions. One way is by changing product standards. Industry standards for products can be "set" by the dominant firm's product. This has been important in the computer industry in preserving IBM's market position. In the early stages of industry development, no effort was made to achieve standardization in areas such as coding data and assigning bits to magnetic tape.[26] This affected the ability of consumers to switch suppliers. Users purchased complete systems; if they desired to switch suppliers, their data and programs were not easily transferrable.[27] As a result of IBM's dominance, its product specifications have become de facto standards. Fringe peripherals producers especially meet IBM's standards and adjust to any product changes which it chooses to make.

Another way in which a firm can alter the supply conditions in its industry is through locking components in a system together, either technologically or through marketing devices. Orthodox theoretical literature suggests that if a firm has a monopoly in one component but not another, linking the two will not constitute an extension of monopoly power since the monopolist will have extracted all monopoly rents in the one market and nothing will remain to be extracted from the competitive market.[28] More recent studies have suggested that if the components can be combined in variable proportions, the monopolist selling in a competitive industry downstream will not be able to reap full monopoly rents.[29] Under these circumstances a monopolist would have an incentive to vertically integrate downstream. Blair and Kaserman in "Vertical Integration, Tying, and Antitrust Policy," further demonstrate that the monopolist could obtain identical results by tying the two products together rather than integrating forward.[30]

Blair and Kaserman's research has implications for dominant firms for which integration may be infeasible. For example, IBM produces CPU's and peripherals, Eastman Kodak produces film and cameras, and Gillette produces razors and blades. In each case their products may be combined in variable proportions to produce the "goods" computing services, photographs, and shaves. Vertical integration by IBM, Kodak, or Gillette into these final product areas is, however, infeasible. Tying of the two components allows them to achieve the same result. Marketing of components as a system is thus another way in which dominant firms can reinforce their market position through altering the nature of the product and its conditions of production.

In summary, the most important way in which firm behavior indirectly generates market structure is through its effect upon demand. Kodak, Procter, Campbell, Gillette, and IBM all owe a large part of their persistence to this factor. Needless to say, it is not sufficient to sustain a dominant position, but in the process of creating demand, product loyalty is also generated. Innovation resulting in new products and, in turn, generating new demand thus plays as important a role in the persistence of dominance as in its creation.

Conclusion

As a means of affecting the development of market structure, non-price policies were used extensively by this sample of firms. The product itself embodies a host of factors that are open to change, and competitors cannot respond as easily or rapidly to non-price as to price changes. As a result, non-price policies had an important impact on the evolution of market structure and persistence of dominance. Entry or expansion by the fringe was made difficult by several discretionary firm actions. Product proliferation strategies, leasing, and systems introductions all contributed to the persistence of the dominant firm. Firm actions, although contributing to persistence, were not necessarily bad from a welfare point of view. Quality, while it differentiates products, is not undesirable, nor is innovation. Just as innovation was important in the creation of the market structure, it was also important in its maintenance although the magnitude of innovation by this sample of firms did not necessarily justify their continuing market power.

The dominant firms played an active role both in the creation of market power and also in its maintenance. Market power could not be retained by Kodak, Gillette, Campbell, IBM, Boeing, and Procter without them actively working to do so. It was, however, lost through passive behavior in the areas of product change and demand creation by Coca-Cola, United Shoe, and Pullman.

7

Conclusions

The objective of this research was to study a sample of dominant firms and to evaluate their behavior in light of predictions by dominant firm models. While examining the sources of dominant firms' market power and their behavioral patterns we have also surveyed the evolution of a market structure. This research revealed how one firm came to acquire a position of dominance and what conduct, if any, contributed to the maintenance of that power.

A dominant firm structure never appeared to be pre-determined. On the contrary, the firms in this sample took an active role in its creation. In two instances market power was achieved solely as a result of active sources of market power, but in the remaining cases both active and passive factors played a role. Although dominance was not inevitable in these latter cases, neither was it entirely at the discretion of the firms' business policies since, for every firm in this sample, at least two factors played a role in its creation. Nor is dominance necessarily easy to establish. Factors such as the type of product, technology of production, manner of distribution, and nature of demand determine the manner and ease with which dominance can be established. Likewise, they determine which competitive strategies are available to the firms for the maintenance of market power.

For firms producing a high technology product, invention or innovation is the most common first step toward the acquisition of dominance. All of the firms in the sample relied on it in some form. An important element in both the creation and maintenance of market power is the ability to control the definition of "the product" in the eyes of the consumers and thus influence the growth of demand. Firms that invent new products can more easily direct demand growth.

Invention alone does not ensure market power; secondary factors are necessary to prevent copying or to deter imitation. Technology and marketing methods generally constrain the supporting factors available for the firm's use. The underlying product technology determines whether the firm is able to realize economies of scale or learning effects. There was evidence that Pullman, Boeing, and IBM relied on one or both of these. To an extent, the conditions of production also determine the usefulness of patents; if the product technology is changing too rapidly, patents are of little value. This was the experience of IBM and Boeing, although Pullman, United Shoe, and Kodak held several patents. The marketing methods chosen, in addition to affecting the growth of demand, may also assist in the creation of product loyalty. The leases of United Shoe served this function, as did Eastman Kodak's network of dealers.

In summary, a strategy for acquiring dominance in a high technology product generally included invention or innovation, the realization of scale economies and development of some form of product loyalty. A variation in this pattern was due largely to the age of the firm. The older firms held some patents or participated in mergers.

Invention or innovation was also of importance in the acquisition of dominance by firms producing branded consumer goods. Their supporting factors were different from those of the high technology producers. Patents or secrecy played a larger role for all firms in this group. Product loyalty was also important for these firms, but they generated it in a manner other than that used by producers of high technology goods. Advertising and emphasis on the quality of the product were more common sources of product loyalty than marketing techniques such as leasing. A strategy for acquiring dominance for this group of firms would generally include invention or innovation coupled with patents or product loyalty or both.

Just as the acquisition of dominance required the active participation of firms, so did its maintenance. Firm conduct determines the evolution of the market structure directly through its effect on number of competitors, barriers to entry, and product differentiation and indirectly through its effect on supply and demand. The same conditions that affected the way in which dominance was acquired also affect the way in which firms can maintain it. Product type, the technology of production, and the nature of demand determine the competitive strategies available to firms for maintenance of dominance.

The main reason for a decline in market power among this sample was an inability to determine the level and direction of demand growth. The two most common means of controlling demand were innovation and product strategies. The more instrumental the dominant firm was in developing new products and organizational forms, the less it had to respond to competitive challenges of this nature from other firms. This does not imply that all firms that maintained their market power were aggressive innovators. Some dominant firms proved to be quick imitators instead. They were generally aided by intangible capital in the form of distribution networks, an established base of customers, and marketing expertise.

The tools available to the firm for directing demand growth differ by product type. The high technology firms use a stream of new products and a succession of product changes. Branded, consumer products firms also introduce new products, but they are more often of the form of new brands or varieties.

An evaluation of the behavior of this sample of firms in light of predictions by dominant firm models reveals that the models do not predict the behavior of the firms very well. Dominant firms do have significantly higher profit than other large firms. One implication of this is that they have more internal funds to use for investment as Schumpeter suggested. In terms of their price policy, however, dominant firms appear to follow neither the limit pricing model nor the price leadership model. They use price as a competitive device but only for short-run strategic moves. Non-price policies in the form of product changes, research and development, and diversification strategies are more common and more important in their long-run effect on competition.

These results have implications for received theory. In particular, the small role that price strategy played suggests that continued emphasis on it in models of firm behavior is unlikely to result in large predictive power. A non-competitive market structure places variables other than price at a firm's discretion. Theory must begin to take this into account. In addition, these results suggest that the form which concentration takes is important in explaining firm behavior. Introduction of a variable for type of market power made a difference in standard profitability-concentration studies. The implications of those particular competitive strategies available to firms also differ by structure. For example, leasing would have different effects in an oligopolistic market structure as opposed to a dominant firm structure since firms with approximately the same resources would be constrained in a similar manner.

This research does not provide anti-trust enforcers with a clear-cut approach to dominant firms. The fact that in every case dominance was the result of at least one active factor suggests it is, in some sense, preventable. However, some of these active factors are not necessarily undesirable. In particular, they include innovation and invention which are legal sources of market power. Passive factors played a role in all but two firms' histories. The relative importance of active versus passive factors in these latter cases is difficult to judge. It does suggest that a fruitful approach would be to examine conduct that serves to support market power. This is the direction in which the courts are moving: given that market power was obtained by legal means they have taken to examining conduct that perpetuates market power. Conduct is the key to the persistence of market power, and it is easily observable. In terms of potential relief, conduct can be prevented by injunction.

Appendix A

Sample Statistics: Data Used in Concentration-Profitability Studies

Variable Name	Mean	Standard Deviation
After tax rate of return on equity (PF)	.1118	.0606
Concentration (CONCEN)	63.1138	17.4817
Log of Assets (LOGA)	5.3917	1.1871
Leverage (LV)	.6453	.1325
Concentration Squared (CSQ)	4286.4797	2222.0577
Dominance Dummy (D)	.1545	.3629
Branded Goods Dummy (BRAND)	.0732	.2615
High Technology Goods Dummy (HITEC)	.0813	.2744

Appendix B

Correlation Coefficients

	PF	CONCEN	LOGA	LV	CSQ	D	BRAND	HITEC
PF	1.0000	.4047	-.0961	-.0329	.3924	.4129	.3787	.1851
CONCEN		1.0000	.0927	-.0125	.9893	.4120	.2600	.2971
LOGA			1.0000	.0231	.0660	.0680	-.0086	.0981
LV				1.0000	.0089	.0070	.0203	-.0101
CSQ					1.0000	.4229	.2672	.3046
D						1.0000	.6574	.6960
BRAND							1.0000	-.0836
HITEC								1.0000

Notes

Chapter 1

1. Archibald J. Nichol, "Partial Monopoly and Price Leadership" (Ph.D. dissertation, Columbia University, 1930).

2. F.M. Scherer, *Industrial Market Structure and Economic Performance* (Chicago: Rand McNally, 1970), pp. 164, 216.

3. Darius W. Gaskins, Jr., "Dynamic Limit Pricing: Optimal Pricing Under Threat of Entry," *Journal of Economic Theory* 3 (1971): 306-22.

4. G.J. Stigler, "The Dominant Firm and The Inverted Umbrella," *Journal of Law and Economics* 8 (October 1965): 167-72; Darius W. Gaskins, Jr., "Optimal Pricing by Dominant Firms" (Ph.D. dissertation, University of Michigan, 1970), pp. 105-10.

5. Oliver E. Williamson, "Dominant Firms and the Monopoly Problem: Market Failure Considerations," *Harvard Law Review* 85 (June 1972): 1512.

6. Scherer, *Industrial Market Structure.*

7. G.J. Stigler, "The Kinky Oligopoly Demand Curve and Rigid Prices," *Journal of Political Economy* 35 (October 1947): 446.

8. By permission. From *Webster's New Collegiate Dictionary,* ©1981 by Merriam-Webster Inc., publisher of the Merriam-Webster® dictionaries.

9. F. Zeuthen, *Problems of Monopoly and Economic Warfare* (London: Routledge & Paul Kegan, Ltd., 1930), p. 17.

10. Fritz Machlup, *The Economics of Sellers' Competition: Model Analysis of Sellers' Conduct* (Baltimore: The Johns Hopkins Press, 1952), p. 404.

11. Using optimal control theory, Gaskins, "Dynamic Limit Pricing," estimates optimal price trajectories for firms under various assumptions about costs and demand.

12. *United States vs. Aluminum Co. of America,* 148 F. 2d 416 (2d Cir. 1945).

13. *U.S. vs. Alcoa,* p. 431.

14. Their 1977 production accounted for 62% of the total U.S. production, as reported in the 1978 *Commodity Year Book,* Harry Jiler, ed., (New York: Commodity Research Bureau, Inc., 1978), p. 232.

15. *United States vs. United Shoe Machinery Corp.,* 110 F. Supp. 295 (D. Mass. 1953), aff'd per curiam, 347 U.S. 521 (1954).

16. *United States vs. United Shoe Machinery Company of New Jersey,* 247 U.S. 32.

17. *U.S. vs. Alcoa.*

18. Scherer, *Industrial Market Structure,* pp. 125-30.

19. *U.S. vs. Alcoa.*

20. Joe S. Bain, "A Note on Pricing in Monopoly and Oligopoly," *American Economic Review* 39 (March 1959): 454.

21. *U.S. vs. Alcoa,* p. 431.

22. A. Michael Spence, "Entry, Capacity, Investment and Oligopolistic Pricing," *Bell Journal of Economics* 8 (Autumn 1977): 541.

23. Joseph A. Schumpeter, *Capitalism, Socialism and Democracy* (New York: Harper, 1942), p. 87.

24. Sherman Anti-Trust Act (Trusts), 2 July 1890, Ch. 647, 26 Stat. 209 (Title 15, paragraphs 1-7).

25. 21 Cong. Rec. 3151-52 (1890).

26. 221 U.S. 1, 60-61 (1911).

27. 221 U.S. 1, 61-62 (1911).

28. 221 U.S. 1, 55-56 (1911).

29. *United States vs. Aluminum Co. of America,* 148 F. 2d 430 (2d. Cir. 1945).

30. *United States vs. American Tobacco Co.,* 221 U.S. 106, 181-83 (1911).

31. 221 U.S. 183 (1911).

32. Phillip Areeda and Donald F. Turner, *Antitrust Law: An Analysis of Antitrust Principles and their Application,* Volume III (Boston: Little Brown and Company, 1978).

33. 251 U.S. 460.

34. 274 U.S. 693.

35. 148 F. 2d 429 (2d. Cir. 1945).

36. 148 F. 2d 430 (2d. Cir. 1945).

37. 148 F. 2d 430 (2d. Cir. 1945).

38. 148 F. 2d 431 (2d. Cir. 1945).

39. 110 F. Supp. 295 (D. Mass. 1953), aff'd per curiam, 347 U.S. 521 (1954).

40. 110 F. Supp. 341 (D. Mass. 1953).

41. 110 F. Supp. 342 (D. Mass. 1953).

42. *United States vs. United Shoe Machinery Co. of N.J.,* 247 U.S. 32.

43. 110 F. Supp. 344-45 (D. Mass. 1953).

44. 110 F. Supp. 344 (D. Mass. 1953).

Chapter 2

1. This chapter may be omitted without affecting understanding of the remaining discussion.

2. Clair Wilcox and William G. Shepherd, *Public Policies Toward Business* (Homewood, IL: Richard D. Irwin, Inc., 1975), p. 47.

3. Leonard W. Weiss, "The Concentration-Profits Relationship and Antitrust," *Industrial Concentration: The New Learning*, Harvey J. Goldschmid, et al., ed., (Boston: Little, Brown and Co., 1974), p. 157.

4. William G. Shepherd, "The Elements of Market Structure," *Review of Economics and Statistics* 54 (February 1972): 25-37. Shepherd cited the following sources in the development of his data: annual company reports, *Moody's Industrials*, the Fortune *Plant and Product Directory of the Largest 1,000 U.S. Industrial Corporations*, 1963-64 and 1965-66, the Fortune *Directory of the 500 Largest U.S. Industrial Corporations*, annual, Standard and Poor's *Industry Reports*, various years, U.S. Senate Subcommittee on Antitrust and Monopoly, *Concentration Ratios in Manufacturing Industry*, 1963, *Part I*, 89th Cong., 2d Sess., 1966, and *Part II*, 90th Cong., 1s Sess., 1967 in addition to various industry studies and trade journals.

5. It is not always possible to identify the next largest firm from Shepherd's data. If this was the case, a firm was included if its market share was at least 50% of the 4-firm concentration ratio.

6. Although we feel Western Electric typifies a dominant firm, it has been eliminated from the sample used in the following statistical investigations because data were only available for American Telephone and Telegraph as a whole.

7. Shepherd's market share estimates were for an early year, 1961. We included Xerox and Procter because we felt they typified dominant firms over the majority of the twenty year period under study. They would "qualify" as dominant firms under market share estimates given by Wilcox and Shepherd for the year 1973.

8. Leonard Weiss, "The Concentration-Profits Relationship and Antitrust," p. 187.

9. After tax rate of return on assets is measured as (net income + interest)/assets.

10. After tax rate of return on equity is measured as (net income)/(common + preferred stock).

11. Schumpeter, *Capitalism, Socialism and Democracy*, p. 87.

12. Betty Bock, *Statistical Games and the "200 Largest" Industrials: 1954 and 1968* (New York: The Conference Board, 1970), pp. 58-72.

13. Leonard Weiss in "The Concentration-Profits Relationship and Antitrust" reviews these studies at some length.

14. Bradley T. Gale, "Market Share and Rate of Return," *Review of Economics and Statistics* 54 (November 1972): 412-23.

15. George J. Stigler, *Capital and Rates of Return in Manufacturing Industries* (Princeton: Princeton University Press, 1963).

16. E. Singer, "Industrial Organization: Price Models and Price Policy," *American Economic Review* 60 (May 1970): 90-99.

17. Y. Brozen, "The Anti-Task Force Deconcentration Recommendation," *Journal of Law and Economics* 13 (October 1970): 279-92; and "Bain's Concentration and Rates of Return Revisited," *Journal of Law and Economics* 14 (October 1971): 351-70.

18. S. Ornstein, "Concentration and Profits." In Weston and Ornstein, eds., *The Impact of Large Firms on the U.S. Economy* (Lexington, Mass.: Lexington Books, 1973), pp. 87-102.

Chapter 3

1. Joseph A. Schumpeter, *Capitalism, Socialism and Democracy* (New York: Harper and Row, 1975), p. 84.

2. Joseph Husband, *The Story of the Pullman Car* (Chicago: A.C. McClurg & Co., 1917), pp. 28-29, 39-40.

3. King Camp Gillette, "Origin of the Gillette Razor," *Gillette Blade,* February 1918, p. 6, quoted in George B. Baldwin, "The Invention of the Modern Safety Razor: A Case Study of Industrial Innovation," *Explorations in Entrepreneurial History* 4 (October 1951-May 1952): 77.

4. Baldwin, "Safety Razor," pp. 78, 81-82, 99.

5. "1068746. Preparing Fruit Products," *Official Gazette of the United States Patent Office* 192 (July 1913): 1114-15; Ira U. Cobleigh, "Soup Stock," *Commercial and Financial Chronicle* 187 (May 29, 1958): 2392.

6. "Eastman Kodak: What Makes it Click?" *Forbes* 91 (April 1, 1963): 23-24.

7. Burton H. Klein, *Dynamic Economics* (Cambridge: Harvard University Press, 1977), pp. 122-28.

8. Charles H. Candler, *Asa Griggs Candler* (Atlanta, Ga.: Emory University, 1950), pp. 176-181.

9. William Rodgers, *Think: A Biography of the Watsons and IBM* (New York: Stein & Day, 1969), p. 199.

10. Gerald W. Brock, *The U.S. Computer Industry: A Study of Market Power* (Cambridge, Mass.: Ballinger Publishing Co., 1975), p. 11.

11. Husband, *Pullman Car,* p. 77.

12. Carl Kaysen, *United States vs. United Shoe Machinery Corporation: An Economic Analysis of an Anti-Trust Case* (Cambridge: Harvard University Press, 1956), pp. 78-79, 85.

13. George Eastman, personal letter to Eastman Photo Materials Co., Ltd., 23 April 1896, quoted in Reese V. Jenkins, *Images and Enterprise: Technology and the American Photographic Industry 1839 to 1925* (Baltimore: The Johns Hopkins University Press, c. 1975), p. 184.

14. Jenkins, *Images,* pp. 90-91, 97, 184.

15. William S. Rukeyser, "Fact and Foam in the Row over Phosphates," *Fortune* 85 (January 1972): 72.

16. Brock, *U.S. Computer Industry,* pp. 28-30.

17. Brock, *U.S. Computer Industry,* pp. 28-30.

18. Sidney L. Carroll, "The Market for Commercial Airlines," *Regulating the Product: Quality and Variety,* ed. Richard E. Caves and Marc J. Roberts, (Cambridge, Mass.: Ballinger Publishing Co., 1975), p. 149.

19. Kaysen, *United Shoe,* pp. 93-97.

20. Simon N. Whitney, *Antitrust Policies: American Experience in Twenty Industries,* 2 (New York: Twentieth Century Fund, 1958), pp. 332-33.

21. J.M. Hoerle, "Campbell Soup Company: Geared to Grow with Nation's Appetite," *Industrial Development and Manufacturers Record* 127 (October 1958): 64-67.

22. "Soup Kitchen of the Nation," *Forbes* 87 (April 15, 1961): 21.

23. Jenkins, *Images* pp. 71-72.

24. Rukeyser, "Fact and Foam," p. 71.

25. P.A.R. Puplett, *Synthetic Detergents: A Study of the Development and Marketing of a New Product* (London: Sidgwick and Jackson, 1957), pp. 54-55, 57.

26. "The P&G Milestones: Candles to Cake Mix," *Dun's Review*, 81, (May 1963): 50; "P&G: What Explains its Success?" *Printers' Ink*, 280, (September 28, 1962): 31.

27. Lawrence Bernard, "Couldn't Compete Without All, Says Lever President," *Advertising Age* 34 (January 21, 1963): 78.

28. Hoerle, "Campbell Soup," pp. 66-67.

29. Securities and Exchange Commission, *Form 10-K, The Gillette Company, for the Fiscal Year Ended December 31, 1977,* Commission File No. 1-922, p. 6; Joan Greene, "Experts in Grime," *Barron's* 47 (24 April 1967): 11.

30. Klein, *Dynamic Economics,* pp. 118, 124.

31. Brock, *U.S. Computer Industry,* p. 63.

32. Jenkins, *Images,* pp. 191-204.

33. Kaysen, *United Shoe,* pp. 6-9, 59-61.

34. Jenkins, *Images,* pp. 190-91.

35. *United States vs. Eastman Kodak Co.,* 266 F. Rep. 75.

36. Jenkins, *Images,* pp. 217-18, 352.

37. *United States vs. Pullman Co.,* 50 F. Supp. 126.

38. *Moody's,* 1978, s.v. "International Business Machines Corp."

39. Brock, *U.S. Computer Industry,* p. 12.

40. *Moody's,* 1975, s.v. "Procter & Gamble."

41. Almarin Phillips, *Technology and Market Structure: A Study of the Aircraft Industry* (Lexington, Mass.: Lexington Books, 1971), p. 83.

42. Husband, *Pullman Car,* pp. 39-40.

43. Candler, *Candler,* pp. 105, 161-65.

44. George Eastman testimony in *United States vs. Eastman Kodak Co.,* 226 F. Rep. 62 (1915). *Abridged Transcript of Record,* pp. 272-73. Appellate Case File No. 25293, Legislative, Judicial, and Diplomatic Records Division, National Archives, Washington, DC. Quoted in Jenkins, *Images,* p. 278.

45. Spencer Klaw, "Soap Wars: A Strategic Analysis," *Fortune* 67 (June 1963): 182.

46. Kaysen, *United Shoe,* pp. 9-10, 74, 77.

47. Brock, *U.S. Computer Industry,* pp. 98-99.

48. Jenkins, *Images*, pp. 195-202.

49. Kaysen, *United Shoe*, pp. 102-12.

50. Whitney, *Antitrust Policies*, 2: 322-23.

51. "Behind Procter & Gamble's Marketing Success," *Dun's Review* 81 (May 1963): 50.

52. Brock, *U.S. Computer Industry*, pp. 13-23, 190-91.

53. Carroll, "Commercial Airlines," pp. 148-49.

54. George Eastman, Letter to Eastman Photo Materials Co., Ltd. 23 April 1896, quoted in Jenkins, *Images*, p. 184.

55. Procter's patent was on Tide's high-phosphate formula. Phosphates serve as a "builder" in detergents and other chemicals may perform this function.

56. Baldwin, "Safety Razor," p. 93.

57. Ira U. Cobleigh, "Soup Stock," *Commercial and Financial Chronicle* 187 (May 29, 1958): 4.

Chapter 4

1. Sidney L. Carroll, "The Market for Commercial Airlines," *Regulating the Product: Quality and Variety,* ed. Richard E. Caves and Marc J. Roberts (Cambridge, Mass.: Ballinger Publishing Co., 1975), p. 150.

2. William H. Gregory, "Rising Costs Delay Jet Transport," *Aviation Week and Space Technology* 72 (May 2, 1960): 77, cited in Carroll, "Commercial Airlines," p. 150.

3. Bootleggers take advantage of these disparities in bottlers' cost and ship Coke from low to high price territories. Bottlers themselves are prevented from doing this. John Koten, "Bootleggers Plague Soft-Drink Industry by Utilizing Differences in Bottlers' Costs," *Wall Street Journal,* Eastern edition, 13 March 1979, p. 17; U.S. Congress, Senate, Subcommittee on Antitrust and Monopoly Hearings, *Exclusive Territorial Allocation Legislation,* 92nd Cong., 2d Sess., 1972 (Washington, D.C.: U.S. Government Printing Office, 1973), p. 63.

4. John Koten, "Some Coca-Cola Bottlers Seek to Make Their Own Syrup for Sale to Restaurants." *Wall Street Journal,* Eastern edition, 27 February 1979, p. 15. Reprinted by permission of the *Wall Street Journal,* © Dow Jones, Inc. (1979). All rights reserved.

5. *Berkey Photo, Inc. vs. Eastman Kodak Co.,* 457 F. Supp. 423n. (1978).

6. David Brand, "Kodak Dominates Field, Rolls up Huge Profits, But Antagonizes Many," *Wall Street Journal,* Eastern edition, 15 November 1972, p. 1; "Eastman Kodak: What Makes it Click?" *Forbes* 91 (April 1, 1963): 24.

7. Peter J. Schuyten, "NCR Unveils Computers to Compete with IBM," *New York Times,* 2 March 1979, Sec. D, p. 4.

8. *Telex Corp. vs. International Business Machines Corp.,* 510 F. 2d 894 (1975).

9. Gerald W. Brock, *The U.S. Computer Industry* (Cambridge, Mass.: Ballinger Publishing Co., 1975), pp. 131-32.

10. Darius W. Gaskins, Jr., "Optimal Pricing by Dominant Firms," (Ph.D. dissertation, University of Michigan, 1970), pp. 12-57.

11. "The Blurry Picture at Eastman Kodak," *Forbes* 114 (September 15, 1974): 83, 86.

12. Gaskins, "Optimal Pricing," pp. 42-52.

13.   George B. Baldwin, "The Invention of the Modern Safety Razor: A Case Study of Industrial Innovation," *Explorations in Entrepreneurial History* 4 (October 1951-May 1952): 95-96n.

14.   *Telex Corp. vs. International Business Machines Corp.,* 367 F. Supp. 304.

Chapter 5

1.   Redbook Magazine, *Household Soaps and Synthetic Detergents: Notes on the Industry and Market* (New York: Redbook Magazine Market Research Department, 1958), p. 23.

2.   "Can Compton Recapture Bigger Market Share for P&G's Tide?" *Printers' Ink* 277 (December 8, 1961): 14.

3.   Frank Biancamano, "Detergents: Biggest Fray of All," *Printers' Ink* 293 (October 28, 1966): 54.

4.   This may also be thought of as "variety" proliferation which will be discussed below. Because the flavors are generally promoted as separate brands rather than varieties of one brand, they are included here.

5.   "Things Go Better with Coke—Pepsi a Strong Contender," *Magazine of Wall Street* 120 (April 15, 1967): 30.

6.   "The Coca-Cola Co." *Forbes* 100 (August 1, 1967): 34.

7.   Campbell Soup Company, *Annual Report Fiscal Year 1977,* pp. 9-10, and Campbell Soup Company, *Annual Report Fiscal Year 1978,* pp. 9-10.

8.   Jack B. Weiner, "Campbell's Recipe for Growth," *Dun's Review* 88 (August 1966): 27.

9.   U.S. Department of Commerce, *The U.S. Photographic Industry 1963-73: An Economic Review* (Washington, D.C.: U.S. Government Printing Office, 1976), p. 8.

10.   Walter Guzzardi, Jr., "Gillette Faces the Stainless Steel Dragon," *Fortune* 68 (July 1963): 242.

11.   "How Gillette Has Put on a New Face," *Business Week,* 1 April 1967, pp. 58-60.

12.   Securities and Exchange Commission, *Form 10-K, The Coca-Cola Company, For the Fiscal Year Ended December 31, 1976,* Commission File No. 1-2217, p. 1.

13.   Kenneth C. Fraundorf, "The Social Costs of Packaging Competition in the Beer and Soft Drink Industries," *Antitrust Bulletin* 20 (Winter 1975): 818-21.

14.   "Things Go Better With Coke," p. 30.

15.   Spencer Klaw, "Soap Wars: A Strategic Analysis," *Fortune* 67 (June 1963): 196.

16.   Peter Vanderwicken, "P&G's Secret Ingredient," *Fortune* 90 (July 1974): pp. 79, 164.

17.   O.B. Butler, "What Marketing Expects from R&D," *Research Management* 19 (January 1976): 8.

18.   Gerald W. Brock, *The U.S. Computer Industry: A Study of Market Power* (Cambridge, Mass.: Ballinger Publishing Co., c. 1975), p. 113-14.

19.   Carl Kaysen, *United States vs. United Shoe Machinery Corporation: An Economic Analysis of an Anti-Trust Case* (Cambridge: Harvard University Press, 1956), pp. 158-60.

20.   Brock, *U.S. Computer Industry,* p. 133.

21.   Ibid., pp. 114-15.

22. Carl Kaysen, *United Shoe,* p. 131.

23. Reese V. Jenkins, *Images and Enterprise: Technology and the American Photographic Industry 1839 to 1925* (Baltimore: The Johns Hopkins University Press, c. 1975), p. 91.

24. Klaw, "Soap Wars," *Fortune,* p. 186.

25. Thomas R. Brooks, "Quality at Kodak," *Dun's Review and Modern Industry* 81 (June 1963): 34, 64-66.

26. Richard Austin Smith, "Gillette Looks Sharp Again," *Fortune* 45 (June 1952): 102-3.

27. William M. Carley, "Gillette Co. Struggles As Its Rivals Slice at Fat Profit Margin," *Wall Street Journal,* Eastern ed., 2 February 1972, p. 14. The format of Gillette's ads is a major Madison Avenue criticism of its advertising policy.

28. Alvin Toffler, "The Competition that Refreshes," *Fortune,* 63 (May 1961): 126-27.

29. "In the Soup and Happy to be There," *Business Week,* 15 February 1964, pp. 126-27.

30. "Consumers Union Says Frozen Breakfast Items Had Insect Body Parts," *Wall Street Journal,* Eastern ed., 1 March 1970, p. 14.

31. "FTC Data Reveal Heinz as One That Blew Whistle on Campbell's Marbles," *Advertising Age* 47 (December 6, 1976): 2, 58.

32. Simon N. Whitney, *Antitrust Policies: American Experience in Twenty Industries,* 2 volumes, (New York: The Twentieth Century Fund, 1958), 2: 332-33.

33. *U.S. vs. Pullman Co.,* 50 F. Supp. 134.

34. Reprinted by permission of the publishers from *United States vs. United Shoe Machinery Corporation: An Economic Analysis of an Anti-Trust Case,* by Carl Kaysen, Cambridge, Mass.: Harvard University Press, Copyright © 1956 by the President and Fellows of Harvard College, p. 184.

35. John J. Riley, *A History of the American Soft Drink Industry* (Washington, D.C.: American Bottlers of Carbonated Beverages, 1958), pp. 138-44.

36. John J. O'Connor, "Schick, Gillette War Sharpens," *Advertising Age* 49 (November 6, 1978): 1.

37. "Soup Kitchen of the Nation," *Forbes* 87 (April 15, 1961): 22, 53; "In the Soup and Happy to be There," *Business Week,* February 15, 1964), p. 133.

38. Jack B. Weiner, "Campbell's Recipe for Growth," *Dun's Review* 88 (August 1966): 45.

39. Jenkins, *Images,* p. 133.

40. Ibid., pp. 203-8.

41. Jenkins, *Images,* pp. 179, 183.

42. John J. O'Connor, "Sylvania, Kodak Cooperate in Debut of Magicube and Instamatic X Camera," *Advertising Age* 41 (July 6, 1970): 38; "GE Unveils the Bulb, Kodak the Cameras in New Pocket Line," *Wall Street Journal,* Eastern ed., 11 April 1975, p. 6; *Berkey Photo, Inc., vs. Eastman Kodak Co.,* 457 F. Supp. 419-421 (1978).

43. "Procter & Gamble," *Forbes* 103 (April 15, 1969): 38.

44. Redbook, *Household Soaps,* pp. 3, 29-31, 39; "Guerrilla War on Soap Giants," *Business Week* 29 August 1964, p. 52.

45. *Telex vs. IBM*, Plaintiff's Exhibit 137, p. 12. Reprinted with permission from Brock, *U.S. Computer Industry: A Study of Market Power*, Copyright 1974, Ballinger Publishing Company, p. 103.

46. Brock, *U.S. Computer Industry*, pp. 148-53.

47. Sidney L. Carroll, "The Market for Commercial Airlines," *Regulating the Product: Quality and Variety*, ed. Richard E. Caves and Marc J. Roberts (Cambridge, Mass.: Ballinger Publishing Co., 1975), pp. 148-49.

48. A. Michael Spence, "Entry, Capacity, Investment and Oligopolistic Pricing," *Bell Journal of Economics* 8 (Autumn 1977).

49. Burton H. Klein, *Dynamic Economics* (Cambridge: Harvard University Press, 1977), p. 126.

50. Peter J. Schuyten, "Big Computer Sector Prospers," *New York Times*, 4 September 1979, p. D4.

51. Louis W. Stern, Oriye Agodo, and Fuat A. Firat, "Territorial Restrictions in Distribution: A Case Analysis," *Journal of Marketing* 40 (April 1976): 70.

52. Michael E. Porter, "How Competitive Forces Shape Strategy," *Harvard Business Review* 57 (March-April 1979): 143.

53. Bill Abrams, "Pepsi, Coke Veterans Launch King-Cola, Plan Soda Pop War," *Wall Street Journal*, Eastern edition, 14 September 1978, p. 16.

54. Jenkins, *Images*, p. 242.

55. Ibid., pp. 242-45.

56. Moody's Industrials, 1974, s.v. "Eastman Kodak."

57. Whitney, *Antitrust Policies*, 2: 219.

58. Securities and Exchange Commission, *Form 10-K, Coca-Cola Company, For the Fiscal Year Ended December 31, 1977*, Commission File No. 1-2217, p. 1.

59. Klein, *Dynamic Economics*, p. 113.

60. John T. Soma, *The Computer Industry: An Economic and Legal Analysis of its Technology and Growth* (Lexington, Mass.: Lexington Books, c. 1976), p. 130.

61. Brock, *U.S. Computer Industry*, p. 194.

62. Peter Vanderwicken, "USM's Hard Life as an Ex-Monopoly," *Fortune* 86 (October 1972): 124-27; "Emhart: Making a Good Fit for USM's Shoe Machinery," *Business Week*, 1 May 1978, pp. 98-103; "Going Barefoot," *Forbes* 96 (November 15, 1965): p. 48.

63. *Moody's Industrials*, 1978, s.v. "Pullman Incorporated."

64. "Gillette: After the Diversification that Failed," *Business Week*, 28 February 1977, p. 59.

65. "How Morgens Make P&G No. 1," *Business Week*, 21 July 1973, p. 49.

66. Carroll, "Commercial Airlines," *Regulating the Product*, pp. 148-49.

67. Kaysen, *United Shoe*, pp. 66-68, 70-71.

68. Brock, *U.S. Computer Industry*, pp. 121-24.

69. *Telex Corp. vs. International Business Machines Corp.*, 367 F. Supp. 292-304.

70. *Telex vs. IBM*, 510 F. 2d 895: *United States vs. United Shoe Machinery Corp.*, Civil No. 7198, District Court of Massachusetts.

71.   *Telex vs. IBM*, 510 F. 2d 927.

72.   Brock, *U.S. Computer Industry*, pp. 130-31.

73.   Robert Sheehan, "The Kodak Picture—Sunshine and Shadow," *Fortune* 71 (May 1965): 152.

Chapter 6

1.   Richard Schmalensee, "Entry Deterrence in the Ready-to-eat Breakfast Cereal Industry," *Bell Journal of Economics* 9 (Autumn, 1978): 305-27.

2.   "How Gillette Has Put on a New Face," *Business Week*, 1 April 1967, pp. 58-69.

3.   "The Sharp Edge of Gillette," *Dun's Review* 89 (April 1967): 67.

4.   "Cheek by Trowel," *Business Week*, 22 December 1962, p. 82.

5.   "Aiding the Enemy," *Forbes* 104 (December 15, 1969): 18.

6.   Spencer Klaw, "Soap Wars: A Strategic Analysis," *Fortune* 67 (June 1963): 191-92, 196.

7.   Redbook Magazine, *Household Soaps and Synthetic Detergents: Notes on the Industry and Market* (New York: Redbook Magazine, Market Research Department, 1958), p. 39.

8.   Lawrence Bernard, "Couldn't Compete Without All Says Lever President," *Advertising Age* 34 (January 21, 1963): 78.

9.   Klaw, "Soap Wars," *Fortune*, pp. 191-92, 196.

10.   Bernard, "Couldn't Compete," *Advertising Age*, p. 78.

11.   Klaw, "Soap Wars," *Fortune*, pp. 191-92, 196.

12.   John Panzer and Robert D. Willig, "Economies of Scale and Economies of Scope in Multi-Output Production," Economic discussion paper, Bell Laboratories, 1975. Cited by Robert D. Willig, "Multiproduct Technology and Market Structure," *American Economic Review* 69 (May 1979): 346.

13.   William J. Baumol and Dietrich Fischer, "Cost-Minimizing Number of Firms and Determination of Industry Structure," *Quarterly Journal of Economics* 20 (August 1978): 439-67.

14.   Gerald W. Brock, *The U.S. Computer Industry: A Study of Market Power* (Cambridge, Mass.: Ballinger Publishing Co., c. 1975), pp. 31-32.

15.   *Berkey Photo, Inc. v. Eastman Kodak Co.*, 457 F.Supp. 415 (1978).

16.   "Eastman Kodak: What Makes It Click?" *Forbes* 91 (April 1, 1963): 22.

17.   "In the Soup and Happy to be There." Quoted from the February 15, 1964 issue of *Business Week* by special permission.

18.   O.B. Butler, "What Marketing Expects from R&D," *Research Management* 19 (January 1976): 9.

19.   George Eastman testimony in *Goodwin Film & Camera Co. vs. Eastman Kodak Co.*, 207 Fed. Rep. 353 (1913), and 213 Fed. Rep. 231 (1914), *Transcript of Record* and *Briefs* cited in Reese V. Jenkins, *Images and Enterprise: Technology and the American Photographic Industry 1839 to 1925* (Baltimore: Johns Hopkins Press, 1975), pp. 111-12.

20.   U.S. Department of Commerce, *The U.S. Photographic Industry 1963-73: An Economic Review* (Washington, D.C.: U.S. Government Printing Office, 1976), p. 8.

21.   "Focus on Change," *Barron's* 45 (April 12, 1965): 5. Reprinted by permission of *Barron's* ©
      Dow Jones & Company, Inc. (1965). All rights reserved.

22.   Brock, *U.S. Computer Industry,* p. 158.

23.   "Gillette New Face," *Business Week,* p. 60.

24.   "Meeting Management Challenges with Imagination," *Nation's Business* 63 (December
      1975): 42-43.

25.   "Business Bulletin," *Wall Street Journal,* Eastern edition, 19 October 1978, p. 1.

26.   For example, a 1960 report on tape drives showed 50 models with tape widths varying from
      1/2 to 2 inches and the number of data tracks varying from 7 to 48. Gerald Brock,
      "Competition Standards and Self-Regulation in the Computer Industry," *Regulating the
      Product: Quality and Variety,* ed. Richard E. Caves and Marc J. Roberts, (Cambridge,
      Mass.: Ballinger Publishing Co., 1975): 77.

27.   Brock, "Competition in the Computer Industry," *Regulating the Product,* pp. 78, 93.

28.   See Robert H. Bork, *The Antitrust Paradox: A Policy at War with Itself* (New York: Basic
      Books, Inc., 1978) for a statement of this position.

29.   David L. Kaserman, "Theories of Vertical Integration: Implications for Antitrust Policy,"
      Antitrust Bulletin 23 (Fall 1978): 483-510, reviews theories of vertical integration at some
      length.

30.   Roger D. Blair and David L. Kaserman, "Vertical Integration, Tying and Antitrust Policy,"
      American Economic Review 68 (June 1978): 397-402.

Bibliography

Books and Articles

Abrams, Bill. "Pepsi, Coke Veterans Launch King-Cola, Plan Soda Pop War." *Wall Street Journal,* Eastern edition, 14 September 1978, p. 16.

"Aiding the Enemy," *Forbes* 104 (December 15, 1969): 18.

Areeda, Phillip, and Turner, Donald F. *Antitrust Law: An Analysis of Antitrust Principles and Their Application.* 3 volumes, Boston: Little Brown and Company, 1978.

Bain, Joe S. "A Note on Pricing in Monopoly and Oligopoly." *American Economic Review* 39 (March 1949): 448-64.

Baldwin, George B. "The Invention of the Modern Safety Razor: A Case Study of Industrial Innovation." *Explorations in Entrepreneurial History* 4 (October 1951-May 1952): 73-102.

Baumol, William J. and Fischer, Dietrich. "Cost-Minimizing Number of Firms and Determination of Industry Structure." *Quarterly Journal of Economics* 20 (August 1978): 439-67.

"Behind P&G's Marketing Success." *Dun's Review* 81 (May 1963): 48.

Bernard, Lawrence. "Couldn't Compete Without All, Says Lever President." *Advertising Age* 34 (January 21, 1963): 1.

_____. "Lever Defense: It was All or Nothing at All." *Advertising Age* 34 (28 January 1963): 1.

Biancamano, Frank. "Detergents: Biggest Fray of All." *Printers' Ink* 293 (October 28, 1966): 53-60.

Blair, Roger D. and Kaserman, David L. "Vertical Integration, Tying and Antitrust Policy." *American Economic Review* 68 (June 1978): 397-402.

"The Blurry Picture at Eastman Kodak." *Forbes* 114 (September 15, 1974): 83-92.

Bock, Betty. *Statistical Games and the "200 Largest" Industrials: 1954 and 1968.* New York: The Conference Board, 1970.

Brand, David. "Kodak Dominates Field Rolls Up Huge Profits, But Antagonizes Many." *Wall Street Journal,* Eastern edition, 15 November 1972, p. 1.

Brock, Gerald W. "Competition Standards and Self-Regulation in the Computer Industry." In *Regulating the Product: Quality and Variety,* pp. 75-96. Edited by Richard E. Caves and Marc J. Roberts. Cambridge, Mass.: Ballinger Publishing Co., 1975.

_____. *The U.S. Computer Industry: A Study of Market Power.* Cambridge, Mass.: Ballinger Publishing Co., c. 1975.

Brooks, Thomas R. "Quality at Kodak." *Dun's Review and Modern Industry* 81 (June 1963): 33.

Brozen, Yale. "The Anti-Task Force Deconcentration Recommendation." *Journal of Law and Economics* 13 (October 1970): 279-92.

_____. "Bain's Concentration and Rates of Return Revisited." *Journal of Law and Economics* 14 (October 1971): 351-70.

Butler, O.B. "What Marketing Expects from R&D." *Research Management* 19 (January 1976): 7-9.

"Can Compton Recapture Bigger Market Share for P&G's Tide?" *Printers' Ink* 277 (December 8, 1961): 14.

Candler, Charles H. *Asa Griggs Candler.* Atlanta, Ga.: Emory University, 1950.

Carley, William M. "Gillette Co. Struggles as Rivals Slice at Fat Profit Margin." *Wall Street Journal,* Eastern edition, 2 February 1972, p. 1.

Carroll, Sidney L. "The Market for Commercial Airlines." In *Regulating the Product: Quality and Variety,* pp. 145-69. Edited by Richard E. Caves and Marc J. Roberts. Cambridge, Mass.: Ballinger Publishing Co., 1975.

"Cheek by Trowel." *Business Week,* 22 December 1962, pp. 81-82.

Cobleigh, Ira U. "Soup Stock." *Commercial and Financial Chronicle* 187 (May 29, 1958): 2392.

"The Coca-Cola Co." *Forbes* 100 (August 1, 1967): 26-34.

"Consumers Union Says Frozen Breakfast Item Had Insect Body Parts." *Wall Street Journal,* Eastern edition, 1 March 1970, p. 14.

Eastman, George. Personal letter to Darragh de Lancey, 29 January 1920. Quoted in Reese V. Jenkins, *Images and Enterprise: Technology and the American Photographic Industry 1839 to 1925,* p. 180. Baltimore: The Johns Hopkins University Press, c. 1975.

_____. Personal letter to Eastman Photo Materials Co., Ltd., 23 April 1896. Quoted in Reese V. Jenkins, *Images and Enterprise: Technology and the American Photographic Industry 1839 to 1925,* p. 184. Baltimore: The Johns Hopkins University Press, c. 1975.

_____. Testimony in *United States vs. Eastman Kodak Co.,* pp. 272-73. Quoted in Reese V. Jenkins, *Images and Enterprise: Technology and the American Photographic Industry 1839 to 1925,* p. 278. Baltimore: Johns Hopkins University Press, c. 1975.

"Eastman Kodak: What Makes It Click?" *Forbes* 91 (April 1, 1963): 22-26.

"Emhart: Making a Good Fit for USM's Shoe Machinery." *Business Week,* 1 May 1978, pp. 98-103.

Fraundorf, Kenneth C. "The Social Costs of Packaging Competition in the Beer and Soft Drink Industries." *Antitrust Bulletin* 20 (Winter 1975): 803-31.

"FTC Data Reveal Heinz as One that Blew Whistle on Campbell's Marbles." *Advertising Age* 47 (December 6, 1976): 2.

Gale, Bradley T. "Market Share and Rate of Return." *Review of Economics and Statistics* 54 (November 1972): 412-23.

Gaskins, Darius W., Jr. "Dynamic Limit Pricing: Optimal Pricing Under Threat of Entry." *Journal of Economic Theory* 3 (1971): 306-22.

_____. "Optimal Pricing by Dominant Firms." Ph.D. dissertation, University of Michigan, 1970.

"GE Unveils the Bulb, Kodak the Cameras in New Pocket Line." *Wall Street Journal,* Eastern edition, 11 April 1975, p. 6.

Greene, Joan. "Experts in Grime." *Barron's* 47 (24 April 1967): 11.

"Gillette: After the Diversification that Failed." *Business Week* 28 February 1977, pp. 58-62.

Gillette, King Camp. "Origins of the Gillette Razor." *Gillette Blade,* February 1918, p. 6. Quoted in George B. Baldwin, "The Invention of the Modern Safety Razor: A Case Study of Industrial Innovation." *Explorations in Entrepreneurial History,* p. 77. 4 (October 1951-May 1952): 73-102.

"Going Barefoot." *Forbes* 96 (November 15, 1965): 48-50.

Gregory, William H. "Rising Costs Delay Jet Transport." *Aviation Week and Space Technology* 72 (May 2, 1960): 77. Cited in Sidney L. Carroll, "The Market for Commercial Airlines." *Regulating the Product: Quality and Variety,* p. 150. Cambridge, Mass.: Ballinger Publishing Co., 1975.

"Guerrilla War on Soap Giants." *Business Week,* 29 August 1964, pp. 50-52.

Guzzardi, Walter, Jr. "Gillette Faces the Stainless-Steel Dragon." *Fortune* 68 (July 1963): 159.

Hoerle, J.M. "Campbell Soup Company: Geared to Grow with Nation's Appetite." *Industrial Development and Manufacturers Record* 127 (October 1958): 64-67.

"How Gillette Has Put on a New Face." *Business Week,* 1 April 1967, pp. 58-66.

"How Morgens Makes P&G No. 1." *Business Week,* 21 July 1973, pp. 48-50.

Husband, Joseph. *The Story of the Pullman Car.* Chicago: A.C. McClung & Co., 1917.

"In the Soup and Happy to be There." *Business Week,* 15 February 1964, pp. 124-33.

Jenkins, Reese V. *Images and Enterprise: Technology and the American Photographic Industry 1839 to 1925.* Baltimore: The Johns Hopkins Press, c. 1975.

Jiler, Harry, ed. *1978 Commodity Year Book.* New York: Commodity Research Bureau, Inc., 1978.

Kaserman, David L. "Theories of Vertical Integration: Implications for Antitrust Policy." *Antitrust Bulletin* 23 (Fall 1978): 483-510.

Kaysen, Carl. *United States vs. United Shoe Machinery Corporation: An Economic Analysis of an Anti-Trust Case.* Cambridge: Harvard University Press, 1956.

Klaw, Spencer. "Soap Wars: A Strategic Analysis." *Fortune* 67 (June 1963): 123.

Klein, Burton H. *Dynamic Economics.* Cambridge: Harvard University Press, 1977.

Koten, John. "Bootleggers Plague Soft-Drink Industry by Utilizing Differences in Bottlers' Costs." *Wall Street Journal,* Eastern edition, 13 March 1979, p. 17.

_____. "Some Coca-Cola Bottlers Seek to Make Their Own Syrup for Sale to Restaurants." *Wall Street Journal,* Eastern edition, 27 February 1979, p. 15.

Machlup, Fritz. *The Economics of Sellers' Competition: Model Analysis of Sellers' Conduct.* Baltimore: The Johns Hopkins Press, 1952.

"Meeting Management Challenges with Imagination." *Nation's Business* 63 (December 1975): 39-46.

Nichol, Archibald J. "Partial Monopoly and Price Leadership." Ph.D. dissertation, Columbia University, 1930.

O'Connor, John J. "Schick, Gillette War Sharpens." *Advertising Age* 49 (November 6, 1978): 1.

_____. "Sylvania, Kodak Cooperate in Debut of Magicube and Instamatic X Camera." *Advertising Age* 41 (July 6, 1970): 39.

Ornstein, Stanley I. "Concentration and Profits." In *The Impact of Large Firms on the U.S. Economy,* pp. 87-102. Edited by J. Fred Weston and Stanley I. Ornstein. Lexington, Mass.: Lexington Books, 1973.

"P&G: What Explains its Success?" *Printers' Ink* 280 (September 28, 1962): 29-45.

"The P&G Milestones: Candles to Cake Mix." *Dun's Review* 81 (May 1963): 50.

Panzar, John and Willig, Robert D. "Economies of Scale and Economies of Scope in Multi-Output Production." Economic discussion paper, Bell Laboratories, 1975.

Phillips, Almarin. *Technology and Market Structure: A Study of the Aircraft Industry.* Lexington, Mass.: Lexington Books, 1971.

Porter, Michael E. "How Competitive Forces Shape Strategy." *Harvard Business Review* 57 (March-April 1979): 137-45.

"Procter & Gamble." *Forbes* 103 (April 15, 1969): 36.

Puplett, P.A.R. *Synthetic Detergents: A Study of the Development and Marketing of a New Product.* London: Sidgwick and Jackson, 1957.

Redbook Magazine. *Household Soaps and Synthetic Detergents: Notes on the Industry and Market.* New York: Redbook Magazine Market Research Department, 1958.

Riley, John J. *A History of the American Soft Drink Industry.* Washington, D.C.: American Bottlers of Carbonated Beverages, 1958.

Rodgers, William. *Think: A Biography of the Watsons and IBM.* New York: Stein & Day, 1969.

Rukeyser, William S. "Fact and Foam in the Row over Phosphates." *Fortune* 85 (January 1972): 71.

Scherer, F.M. *Industrial Market Structure and Economic Performance.* Chicago: Rand McNally, 1970.

Schmalensee, Richard. "Entry Deterrence in the Ready-to-Eat Breakfast Cereal Industry." *Bell Journal of Economics* 9 (Autumn 1978): 305-27.

Schumpeter, Joseph A. *Capitalism, Socialism and Democracy.* New York: Harper, 1942.

Schuyten, Peter J. "Big Computer Sector Prospers." *New York Times,* 4 September 1979, p. D1.
_____. "NCR Unveils Computers to Compete with IBM." *New York Times,* 2 March 1979, p. D1.
"The Sharp Edge of Gillette." *Dun's Review* 89 (April 1967): 43.
Sheehan, Robert. "The Kodak Picture-Sunshine and Shadow." *Fortune* 71 (May 1965): 127.
Shepherd, William G. "The Elements of Market Structure." *Review of Economics and Statistics* 54 (February 1972): 25-37.
Singer, Eugene M. "Industrial Organization: Price Models and Price Policy." *American Economic Review* 60 (May 1970): 90-99.
Smith, Richard Austin. "Gillette Looks Sharp Again." *Fortune* 45 (June 1952): 100.
Soma, John T. *The Computer Industry: An Economic and Legal Analysis of its Technology and Growth.* Lexington, Mass.: Lexington Books, c. 1976.
"Soup Kitchen of the Nation." *Forbes* 87 (April 15, 1961): 19-23.
Spence, A. Michael. "Entry, Capacity, Investment and Oligopolistic Pricing." *Bell Journal of Economics* 8 (Autumn 1977): 534-44.
Stern, Louis W., Agodo, Oriye, and Firat, Fuat A. "Territorial Restrictions in Distribution: A Case Analysis." *Journal of Marketing* 40 (April 1976): 69-75.
Stigler, George J. *Capital and Rates of Return in Manufacturing Industries.* Princeton: Princeton University Press, 1963.
_____. "The Dominant Firm and the Inverted Umbrella." *Journal of Law and Economics* 8 (October 1965): 167-72.
_____. "The Kinky Oligopoly Demand Curve and Rigid Prices." *Journal of Political Economy* 35 (October 1947): 432-49.
"Things Go Better with Coke—Pepsi a Strong Contender." *Magazine of Wall Street* 120 (April 15, 1967): 29.
Toffler, Alvin. "The Competition that Refreshes." *Fortune* 63 (May 1961): 124.
Vanderwicken, Peter. "P&G's Secret Ingredient." *Fortune* 90 (July 1974): 75.
_____. "USM's Hard Life as an Ex-Monopoly." *Fortune* 86 (October 1972): 124-30.
Weiner, Jack B. "Campbell's Recipe for Growth." *Dun's Review* 88 (August 1966): 27.
Weiss, Leonard W. "The Concentration-Profits Relationship and Anti-Trust." In *Industrial Concentration: The New Learning,* pp. 184-233. Edited by Harvey J. Goldschmid, H. Michael Mann, and J. Fred Weston. Boston: Little, Brown and Co., 1974.
Whitney, Simon N. *Antitrust Policies: American Experience in Twenty Industries.* 2 volumes, New York: Twentieth Century Fund, 1958.
Wilcox, Clair, and Shepherd, William G. *Public Policies Toward Business.* Homewood, IL: Richard D. Irwin, Inc., 1975.
Williamson, Oliver E. "Dominant Firms and the Monopoly Problem: Market Failure Considerations." *Harvard Law Review* 85 (June 1972): 1512-31.
Willig, Robert D. "Multiproduct Technology and Market Structure." *American Economic Review* 69 (May 1979): 346-51.
Zeuthen, F. *Problems of Monopoly and Economic Warfare.* London: George Routledge & Sons Ltd., 1930.

Legal Cases

American Tobacco vs. United States. 328 U.S. 781 (1946).
Berkey Photo, Inc. vs. Eastman Kodak Co. 457 F. Supp. 404 (1978).
Standard Oil Co. of New Jersey et al. vs. United States. 221 U.S. 1 (1911).
Telex Corp. vs. International Business Machines Corp. 510 F. 2d 894 (1975).
Telex Corp. vs. International Business Machines Corp. 367 F. Supp. 258.
United States vs. Aluminum Co. of America. 148 F. 2d 416 (2d Cir. 1945).
United States vs. American Tobacco Co. 221 U.S. 106 (1911).

United States vs. Eastman Kodak Co. 266 F. Rep. 75.
United States vs. International Harvester Co. et al. 274 U.S. 693.
United States vs. Pullman Co. 50 F. Supp. 126.
United States vs. United Shoe Machinery Corp. Civil No. 7198, District Court of Massachusetts.
United States vs. United Shoe Machinery Corp. 110 F. Supp. 295 (D. Mass. 1953), aff'd per curiam, 347 U.S. 521 (1954).
United States vs. United Shoe Machinery Company of New Jersey. 247 U.S. 32.
United States vs. United States Steel Corp. 251 U.S. 417.

Miscellaneous

"1068746. Preparing Fruit Products." *Official Gazette of the United States Patent Office* 192 (July 1913): 1114-15.
"Annual Report." Various companies and various years.
Moody's Industrial Manual. Various years.
Securities and Exchange Commission. *Form 10-K.* Various companies and various years.
U.S. Congress, Senate, Subcommittee on Antitrust and Monopoly Hearings. *Exclusive Territorial Allocation Legislation.* 92nd Congress, 2d Session, 1972. Washington, D.C.: U.S. Government Printing Office, 1973.
U.S. Department of Commerce. *The U.S. Photographic Industry 1963-73: An Economic Review.* Washington, D.C.: U.S. Government Printing Office, 1976.

Index